ULTIMATE GUIDE

WALKS, PATIOS & WALLS

ULTIMATE GUIDE
WALKS, PATIOS & WALLS

CREATIVE HOMEOWNER®

ULTIMATE GUIDE: WALKS, PATIOS & WALLS

SENIOR EDITOR	Kathie Robitz
GRAPHIC DESIGNER	Kathryn Wityk
PHOTO COORDINATOR	Mary Dolan
JUNIOR EDITOR	Angela Hanson
PROOFREADER	Sara M. Markowitz
DIGITAL IMAGING SPECIALIST	Frank Dyer
INDEXER	Schroeder Indexing Services
COVER DESIGN	Kathryn Wityk
FRONT COVER PHOTOGRAPY	(right, top left & center left)
Jerry Pavia, (bottom left) Todd	Caverly/Brian Vanden Brink
	Photos, design: George Snead, Jr.
BACK COVER PHOTOGRAPY	John Parsekian/CH

Manufactured in China

Current Printing (last digit)
10 9 8 7 6

Ultimate Guide: Walks, Patios & Walls, Third Edition
Library of Congress Control Number: 2009933308
ISBN: 978-1-58011-484-4

We are always looking for talented authors. To submit an idea,
please send a brief inquiry to acquisitions@foxchapelpublishing.com.

Creative Homeowner®, *www.creativehomeowner.com*, is an imprint of
New Design Originals Corporation and distributed exclusively in North America
by Fox Chapel Publishing Company, Inc., 800-457-9112, 903 Square Street,
Mount Joy, PA 17552, and in the United Kingdom by Grantham Book Service,
Trent Road, Grantham, Lincolnshire, NG31 7XQ.

safety

Although the methods in this book have been reviewed for safety, it is not possible to overstate the importance of using the safest methods you can. What follows are reminders—some do's and don'ts of work safety—to use along with your common sense.

- Always use caution, care, and good judgment when following the procedures described in this book.
- Always be sure that the electrical setup is safe, that no circuit is overloaded, and that all power tools and outlets are properly grounded. Do not use power tools in wet locations.
- Always read container labels on paints, solvents, and other products; provide ventilation; and observe all other warnings.
- Always read the manufacturer's instructions for using a tool, especially the warnings.
- Use hold-downs and push sticks whenever possible when working on a table saw. Avoid working short pieces if you can.
- Always remove the key from any drill chuck (portable or press) before starting the drill.
- Always pay deliberate attention to how a tool works so that you can avoid being injured.
- Always know the limitations of your tools. Do not try to force them to do what they were not designed to do.
- Always make sure that any adjustment is locked before proceeding. For example, always check the rip fence on a table saw or the bevel adjustment on a portable saw before starting to work.
- Always clamp small pieces to a bench or other work surface when using a power tool.
- Always wear the appropriate rubber gloves or work gloves when handling chemicals, moving or stacking lumber, working with concrete, or doing heavy construction.
- Always wear a disposable face mask when you create dust by sawing or sanding. Use a special filtering respirator when working with toxic substances and solvents.
- Always wear eye protection, especially when using power tools or striking metal on metal or concrete; a chip can fly off, for example, when chiseling concrete.
- Never work while wearing loose clothing, open cuffs, or jewelry; tie back long hair.
- Always be aware that there is seldom enough

time for your body's reflexes to save you from injury from a power tool in a dangerous situation; everything happens too fast. Be alert!
- Always keep your hands away from the business ends of blades, cutters, and bits.
- Always hold a circular saw firmly, usually with both hands.
- Always use a drill with an auxiliary handle to control the torque when using large-size bits.
- Always check your local building codes when planning new construction. The codes are intended to protect public safety and should be observed to the letter.
- Never work with power tools when you are tired or when under the influence of alcohol or drugs.
- Never cut tiny pieces of wood or pipe using a power saw. When you need a small piece, saw it from a securely clamped longer piece.
- Never change a saw blade or a drill or router bit unless the power cord is unplugged. Do not depend on the switch being off. You might accidentally hit it.
- Never work in insufficient lighting.
- Never work with dull tools. Have them sharpened, or learn how to sharpen them yourself.
- Never use a power tool on a workpiece—large or small—that is not firmly supported.
- Never saw a workpiece that spans a large distance between horses without close support on each side of the cut; the piece can bend, closing on and jamming the blade, causing saw kickback.
- When sawing, never support a workpiece from underneath with your leg or other part of your body.
- Never carry sharp or pointed tools, such as utility knives, awls, or chisels, in your pocket. If you want to carry any of these tools, use a special-purpose tool belt that has leather pockets and holders.

Contents

Introduction

WALKS, PATIOS, AND WALLS turn outdoor areas into usable living spaces. Walks connect the focal points of your yard, both physically and visually. A patio links your house and yard, providing outdoor living, eating, cooking, and entertainment spaces. A brick, stone, or block wall adds character and privacy.

This book will help you get started creating these structures for your yard. An extensive design section aids in laying out your property and planning your project. The section also deals with the practical matters of drainage, and sun and climate control.

The rest of the book is devoted to helping you design and build the projects that will increase the value of your home and make your yard more livable. Grouped into sections that cover walks, patios, and walls, each chapter covers a specific type of structure. Each section contains dozens of design ideas that you can use in your own yard. The projects themselves are the most popular among homeowners and designers. The materials and tools needed to complete them are readily available. The instructions provided here are simple and straightforward. Each sequence lists the tools and materials you will need to do the job and easy-to-follow directions for completing the projects.

GUIDE TO SKILL LEVEL

 Easy. Even for beginners

 Challenging. Can be done by beginners who have the patience and willingness to learn.

 Difficult. Can be handled by most experienced do-it-yourselfers who have mastered basic construction skills. Consider consulting a specialist.

Greenery allowed to grow between the stones of this patio enhances the natural look of the design, above.

Rough-cut stone adds a rustic charm to the walls and walks around this house, opposite.

This stone walk guides you through the garden without feeling formal, top right.

A fun, tropical feel is achieved through the bold color of this brick patio, right.

design basics

1

GOOD LANDSCAPE DESIGN requires a blend of elements. There are technical considerations dictated by the site and your budget, and creative possibilities determined by how you plan on using the landscape. Each site is unique and offers its own challenges, especially when it comes to hardscapes such as walls, walks, and patios. But there are basic principles you can follow that will help you create a design that meets your needs.

YOUR SITE, YOUR LIFESTYLE

In many ways, the concept of site design goes back a long time. The Romans called it *genius loci*—spirit of place. When designed correctly, a place affects all of our senses by providing a combination of sights, sounds, smells, textures, and temperatures. A place is memorable; we can return to it again and again in our minds whenever we want. We all have special places that we hold dear. A good site design can and should provide a memorable experience for all who visit that particular place. Essentially, there are two factors for you to consider as you begin the design process: your site's features and how to enhance them.

Identifying. Your first order of business should be recognizing the unique combination of elements that your site has to offer. These could be such things as special views and vistas; natural features such as trees, rocks, or streams; or even historical artifacts or events that occurred there in the past. Any and all of these will add up to the unique spirit of your particular location. Spend some time getting acquainted with your landscape and noting these special features. Every site has something to tell you.

Intensifying. Once you feel that you understand the special qualities and elements of your site, think of ways in which these features can be preserved and, better yet, enhanced through the placement of such things as walks, walls, patios, and vegetation.

A low wall, above, helps to contain a hilly site without obstructing the view. Plants soften the look.

A walkway constructed of native stone, left, helps to connect a home to its geographic location.

Locating outdoor living spaces, opposite, to take advantage of views enhances relaxation and open-air activities.

Working with Your Surroundings

If your site is in a historic district or an architecturally distinct region—New England or the Southwest come to mind—your design will fit into these contexts if you make an effort to work with the prevailing materials, colors, and architectural elements. This doesn't necessarily mean copying or mimicking every little detail you can find in your neighborhood. There's still plenty of latitude here to design your personal interpretation of what you think makes your region or neighborhood unique. Of course, the choice of whether or not you want to fit into or stand out from your surroundings is entirely up to you. In fact, with so many of today's newer houses looking the same as others in the neighborhood, this is the perfect opportunity to express your personal values and tastes.

One design concept popular in landscape planning involves creating designs that are "of the site" versus those that are not. A design that is considered of the site appears to grow or spring directly from what is already a part of the site, as if the new design were always meant to be there. Frank Lloyd Wright liked to call this "organic design."

Imported Designs. The opposite of an "of the site" design is one that seems to come from somewhere else, such as a New England Cape Cod house in the middle of the Sonora Desert. Although most professional site designers prefer the more organic approach, that doesn't mean you can't incorporate a Japanese Zen rock and sand garden into your design if you wish. It simply means not forcing something onto the site that seems unnatural or incongruous. However, it's best to work with the site.

FORMAL OR INFORMAL?

CONSIDER WHETHER YOU WANT a formal layout; a relaxed, informal layout; or some combination of both. Consider the size and shape of your lot, the style of the house, and your lifestyle. Formal layouts are usually symmetrical and uniform, whereas informal layouts are typically asymmetrical with irregular or naturally flowing shapes. Some of the most satisfying site plans have aspects of both.

Combining informal and formal elements in close proximity enhances and strengthens both through their contrasts. For example, you might try a formal patio layout integrated into a system of informal curvilinear walks, walls, and planting areas. But remember that informal doesn't mean random or chaotic. An underlying sense of balance is just as important to informal layouts as it is to formal layouts. Base a curving walk or wall on circles, radii, and tangents, not just careless squiggles across your site.

In terms of material and design, this patio, opposite, is an extension of its California Mission-style home.

A somewhat formal look has been achieved with this symmetrical design, below left.

A wall composed of random rocks and a crushed-stone path, below, have a rustic, casual appeal.

A yard that isn't perfectly flat isn't necessarily an obstacle to building a patio. This is a slightly hilly location, but with some site grading, it became an idyllic spot for grillin' and chillin'.

Design Basics

Positive and Negative Spaces. Site designers often talk about creating positive and negative spaces. This is a simple yet extremely important aspect of designing a good site. Positive space refers to well-defined and enclosed spaces, while negative space refers to poorly defined spaces and/or spaces with little or no sense of enclosure. Think of trying to drink out of a good, solid coffee mug versus a sieve. Positive spaces, with well-defined borders and edges—walls or walkways, for example—help to gather and contain as well as define spaces. They have a feeling of reaching around and embracing you. Negative spaces, on the other hand, tend to leak and flow out and away from you. As human beings, we tend to find negative or shapeless spaces much less satisfying than well-defined, positive spaces.

Enclosure. The best site designs provide varying degrees of enclosure. A good way to think of enclosure is in

An excellent example of a positive space, above left, features a walkway and borders.

Tucked into a corner, the patio, above right, has a sense of privacy and security.

An undulating shape makes this tall wall, opposite, feel less imposing while it carries the eye along the site.

terms of shelter—how much we are protected from the elements and how much the enclosure provides a sense of privacy and intimacy. A sense of enclosure or positive space is really very simple to achieve, but it certainly does not mean an airtight box. After all, you want to be outdoors to enjoy a free, open feeling. To achieve a satisfying degree of enclosure, a low wall along the edge of a planting area or along the side of a walk—even the edge of a patio with one or more low planters—is all you need.

A Sense of Security. Perhaps you remember how pleasant and secure it felt to sit on the front porch of your grandparents' house in the summertime, or maybe you have another special place that gave you a feeling of security. Ever wish you could re-create that feeling? Well, you can. The people who study these types of things say that humans have a natural tendency to seek slightly elevated and sheltered places and to avoid open, exposed places whenever possible. The slight elevation allows you to see farther in all directions, and the semi-open shelter provides you with a sense of security and allows you to watch and participate in the passing world. Whether it's in your front or backyard, you can create this sense of security by elevating your patio slightly above the surrounding grade, providing a sense of enclosure with a few low walls and planters, and perhaps adding an overhead trellis or patio roof to provide shade and rain protection. Voila! Time to make some lemonade.

Outdoor Scale. A quick note about outdoor scale versus indoor scale. No rocket science here, folks. Outdoor spaces need to be scaled up from the typical dimensions used for rooms inside. If you are using an average-size room inside your house to get a feel for the size of your new patio, add a few extra feet to the dimensions, if possible. What seems like a perfectly adequate space inside can feel uncomfortably cramped and small when it is outside.

And you thought you weren't going to get a good reason for making that new patio just a little bit larger!

FORCING PERSPECTIVE

HERE ARE A COUPLE OF NEAT TRICKS to use when working with small spaces. The perceived size of a space can be increased by slightly narrowing the far end of the area in relation to the width of the end nearest the viewer. This is called forced perspective, and it is a trick that landscape designers learned from painters. It works because our eyes trick our brains into thinking that the space is longer than it really is. You can create this type of perspective by placing larger or taller trees or shrubs in the foreground of a space and then placing smaller, shorter trees or shrubs toward the far end of the space.

Design Basics

Varying Texture. Use fine and coarse textures to increase (or decrease) your perception of spatial depth. Think
about standing on a small mountaintop and looking out
into the distance. You can see every leaf on the trees and
shrubs near you. Then, as you look farther out into the distance, the leaves begin to blur until you can no longer per-
ceive individual leaves or even individual trees. By varying
the textures of the vegetation and/or the wall surfaces in
small spaces, from coarse at the near end to finely textured
at the far end, you can trick your eyes into thinking that the
space is larger than it really is. The reverse is also true (just
in case you want to make a large space look smaller).

smart tip
STEAL SOME IDEAS

Don't be afraid to borrow ideas and designs from friends and neighbors. Most
people find it flattering when someone
copies them. It is also a good way for you
to learn about potential maintenance
problems and long-term life-cycle costs.

BASIC SITE DESIGN

To get to the point where you can put your ideas onto a site drawing, you will first have to understand some basic techniques and terms. Don't worry if you don't grasp the terms immediately. Read through the next section before attempting a design. As you work on your plan, you will find that terms and ideas will become apparent to you.

Design Techniques

These basic design techniques are more or less common to all design professions, including artists.

Small rock plants, tucked between the slabs of a walkway, opposite, vary the texture from hard to soft.

Mexican tiles border a mosaic walkway, above, that comprises shards of flat stone.

Balance. Arrange various site elements so that they are resolved and balanced. A visually heavy or larger object can be balanced by a lighter or smaller one that is darker in color, is unusually or irregularly shaped, is contrasting in texture, or is more elaborately detailed.

These strategies help to draw attention to the smaller object and visually balance it with the larger one. For example, let's say you have a large clump of conifer trees on one side of your yard. To visually balance them, you might plant smaller, more colorful ornamental trees on the other side of the yard, or you might install a man-made object, such as a fountain or a gazebo.

OTHER CONSIDERATIONS

HERE ARE A FEW ADDITIONAL POINTS to consider as you attempt to find the right location for your project.

Site Repair. Rather than picking the nicest spot in your backyard to locate your new patio or other site improvements, choose an area that could stand some enhancement or repair.

Maintenance. It goes without saying that maintenance is an important consideration, especially outdoors. Once your new patio and walks are constructed, it's time to take care of them. Obviously, it pays to select durable and easily cleaned materials, but keep in mind that your design can also create headaches when it comes to cleaning, raking, sweeping, and shoveling snow. Odd angles and tight corners might increase your cleaning tasks. If you live in snow country, ask yourself where you will pile the snow, and plan accordingly.

Life-Cycle Costs. Over the long run, the cheapest materials may turn out to be the most expensive if they need to be replaced or repaired often. For example, if you have 100 square feet of a material that costs $3 per square foot and it needs to be totally replaced every five years, the annual replacement cost will be $60 (100 square feet x $3 = $300 divided by 5 years). On the other hand, if you pick a material that costs $4.50 per square foot and it needs to be replaced every 10 years, the annual replacement cost will only be $45 (100 square feet x $4.50 = $450 divided by 10 years).

Harmony. Harmony can be achieved by selecting and using elements that share a common trait or characteristic. By using elements that are similar in size, shape, color, material, texture, or detail, you can create a cohesive feeling and relation among the various elements on the site. An example of this might be a brick patio that is bordered by a brick planter near a brick walkway leading to a brick-lined garden area. In this case, the various elements are made of a common material. Another example might be using a common shape, such as a square. Imagine having a square concrete patio scored in a square (or diamond) pattern with a square table, square chairs, and a square-checkered tablecloth. The results can be extremely pleasing.

Unity and Variety. While both balance and harmony are used to achieve unity, too much unity can be boring. That's where variety and contrast come in handy. By varying size, shape, color, material, texture, and detail, you can introduce a note of interest or a focal point into the total composition. For instance, placing a round wooden planter onto the square-pattern patio discussed earlier will provide a pleasing contrast of both shape and material. The contrasting object (the round wooden planter) will draw attention to itself and provide a degree of visual relief and interest to the total setting. This is the right time

and place to add your individual touch, including a bit of whimsy or humor if that feels right. However, too much variety can be worse than too much unity and result in a confusing, chaotic jumble. When introducing variety into your plan layout, it's probably better to lean toward the conservative side.

Rhythm. In design terms, rhythm—or the spacing of elements relative to similar elements—can create another type of unity in a composition. Rhythm helps to establish a visually satisfying progression or sequence to a site design. For example, on a walkway, you can establish a regular rhythm if you place a band of decorative brick at 4-foot intervals. This acts as both a control joint and as a source of visual rhythm. Or as another example, you can place pilasters or half-columns along a brick or masonry wall at regular intervals. On the other hand, a song composed of only one sequence of notes is boring. You can avoid visual boredom by varying such things as the interval, color, size, shape, texture, or material of the elements you use to create your sequence. Another fun way to introduce an interesting visual rhythm is to create subsets of elements between the evenly spaced elements. You could also install a series of colorful glazed tiles with their own rhythmic sequence between regularly spaced pilasters of a brick or masonry wall.

Color is an important unifying factor. The color of the stone links the wall to the evenly spaced face and foundation of the house, opposite.

Keep rhythm in mind, particularly if you will be installing a long wall. Concrete pilasters keep the eye moving and look refined in contrast to the rough-cut stone face of this wall, left.

Design Basics

Emphasis. A lot like unity and variety, emphasis assumes that within your site some of the elements have more significance or importance than the rest and that these special elements should be somehow identified as such. You can emphasize an element in any one of a number of ways, including making it larger than other elements, placing it among items that have a different shape, centering it within a circle or at the end of a walkway, or highlighting it at night with floodlights or accent lights. But as with unity and variety, if you emphasize everything then nothing is really emphasized and you end up with a chaotic, visually confusing site design. Use this one with caution.

Simplicity. Don't be fooled. Just because simplicity is the last item on the list doesn't mean it's the least important. In fact, to many designers it's probably the most im-portant concept of all—and you thought this was going to be complicated! Ironically, simplicity is also one of the hardest things to achieve in any design concept. That's because when you realize how many design tools and elements you have to work with, you have a natural tendency to want to use all of them.

Remember trying to mix every color in your new water-color set together just to see what that color would look like? Remember the results? In virtually every case, the most elegant and satisfying site designs are those that begin and end with simplicity as a guiding design princi-ple. The Zen rock gardens of Japan are perhaps the best example of this way of designing—so much is said with so little effort. And that's probably because so much is left to our own individual interpretations. Subtlety and simplicity are good words to remember.

Evenly cut stone slabs installed tightly in a horizontal pattern make a simple but strong statement on this patio, opposite.

Low walls and walkways surrounding the patio and pool, above, help to define and connect the various outdoor living areas of this home.

smart tip

PLAN FOR THE FUTURE

THE WAYS IN WHICH YOU USE YOUR NEW PATIO WILL HELP DETERMINE ITS VALUE. DON'T FORGET TO ADD SOME AMENITIES, SUCH AS A LIGHTING SYSTEM, AN OUTDOOR ELECTRICAL RECEPTACLE, SPACE FOR A GRILL, STORAGE FOR PATIO FURNITURE, AND ROOM TO ADD A SPA OR HOT TUB LATER.

DIVIDING YOUR DESIGN INTO SPECIFIC PARTS

THERE IS MORE TO A DESIGN, however, than the actual physical parts and conceptual places of any given site. To help you arrive at your overall plan, you will have to juggle the following design elements.

Centers. Centers are gathering areas where people come together for a common purpose. We are typically drawn to centers because of their location or placement on the site and their sense of importance within the design. On a larger scale, some examples of centers might be the town square in a traditional New England village or even Rockefeller Center in New York. For our purposes, the obvious example of a center is the patio you are about to design. What are some of the social activities you intend to accommodate in your new patio?

Edges. Edges can be thought of as the linear boundaries between distinctly different areas. Edges can take many forms: natural features, such as streams and rows of shrubs, or man-made elements, such as walls. Low walls, such as the ones illustrated in this book, provide very effective edges that separate areas in a yard, such as planting beds and lawns. Edges give these areas a crisp definition that is much more aesthetically pleasing than unclear, poorly defined boundaries.

Districts. Districts can also be thought of as areas, zones, or fields. For our purposes, examples of districts might include lawn areas, flower beds, play areas, gardens, and especially patios.

Paths. Paths are the obvious complements to the areas of your site. Paths or, better yet, walks connect the outdoor rooms of your site together and make them usable and accessible, and therefore deserve a high degree of thought and consideration on your part.

Nodes. Nodes are basically the same as centers, except that they are more closely associated with walks. You might also think of them as intersections or crossroads. Because intersections are typically busy places when there is a lot of traffic, consider enlarging the major nodes or intersections of your site plan to accommodate passing room or the occasional impromptu conversation.

Organizing Your Site Design

So how are you going to organize all the elements of your site? That's where the use of one or more ordering systems can help make sense of it all. These are the planning tools we can use to gather and arrange the physical places of your site into a cohesive, unified whole instead of a haphazard assortment of unrelated spaces.

Keep in mind, though, that using an ordering system doesn't exclude variety, spontaneity, and points of emphasis within your plan. Also, you might consider using more than one ordering system, depending on which element or place you're designing. For example, a grid system might work best when you are laying out the walls for a lawn and garden area; then you might switch to a symmetrical layout for the patio and to an axial layout for the walks. Impress your friends and neighbors, not to mention your family. Let's see what's in the planning toolbox.

Axes. An axis is an imaginary yet powerful line. You can arrange your outdoor rooms or the lineal elements such as walks and walls on either side of an axis to achieve a sense of balance. An axis will end either in a panoramic view or with a symmetrical vertical element such as a statue, a fountain, or an arbor. Walks and sight lines are good places to use an axial layout.

Grids. Grids can be useful in site design. For example, you might think of your yard as a nine-square grid. When planning your layout, you might overlay this grid on your site to organize such elements as patios, play areas, gardens, and a gazebo. In arranging elements in your grid, consider such factors as traffic patterns, views, and the path of the sun over the yard.

Stone tiles unify a multifunctional patio, opposite. Evenly spaced individual tiles on the ground make a visually interesting walkway.

A soaring chimney serves as the endpoint of the axis layout in this patio's design, top.

Pathways intersect at a center fountain in a European-inspired garden, right.

Hierarchy. You will use hierarchy to rank spaces and elements by order of importance. Every site plan has certain spaces that are more important than others. Think of it this way: normally, the living room is a far more important space than the utility room. You put your best furnishings and carpets and the most money into the living room—not the utility room. Your priorities are up to you, but it's a good bet that your new patio is probably going to be the most important space you are planning. You can give your important spaces the amount of attention they deserve by making them larger than the other spaces. By giving them an unusual or unique shape (for example, a round space within a square grid), or by locating the space in a prominent position, such as the center of your site or at the end of an axis.

Datum. A datum is a reference point, or more accurately, a reference line or plane. An axis is a datum in that it gives elements on either side of it a common line of reference. Walls make good datum lines. Their presence and continuity often help emphasize unique elements. For example, a fence could act as a datum to emphasize plantings of various shapes. Interestingly enough, grids also make good datum lines, as when you overlay a variety of differently shaped objects on a regular pattern. The grid holds everything together.

BASIC GEOMETRY

GEOMETRIC SHAPES are always fun to use when designing just about anything, especially site plans. The basic geometric shapes are the circle, square, and triangle. With these shapes, combined with the other ordering systems, you can design just about everything that comes along. Interesting geometric variations include overlapping the basic shapes to form a third shape (or space) and creating spiral or pinwheel compositions. All of these geometric systems can be combined, overlapped, rotated, and shifted relative to each other and themselves for added variety and complexity. In your yard, the geometric elements might be a triangular trellis, rectangular patios, and round shrubs.

Arranging stone tiles in a grid gives this patio, opposite, a modern look.

A compass rose surrounded by tile, right, draws attention to the area in front of the patio's focal point—a fireplace—and provides a logical axis around which to arrange furniture.

The edge of the patio, below, keeps the circle created by the landscaping uninterrupted. Notice how the low shrubs in front of the tall trees play with perspective.

planning your site 2

BEFORE YOU CAN APPLY THE DESIGN PRINCIPLES covered in the previous chapter, you need to familiarize yourself with some of the more mundane, yet important, aspects of landscape design. Soil, drainage patterns, and grading are extremely important to your final design. Even the most beautiful patio won't be pleasant to use if it's underwater; carefully laid-out walks won't function if they turn into rivers of mud when it rains; and retaining walls won't serve their purpose if they crack and topple over.

SOIL

Soils have three main properties that you should note: the bearing (structural) capacity, the drainage characteristics, and the fertility (ability to support plant life). Soils are divided into two major classifications, depending on the size of the soil particles. There are coarse-grained soils, such as gravel and sand, and fine-grained soils, such as clays and silts.

For both structural and drainage purposes, the coarse-grained soils are preferable. As you can imagine, coarse-grained soils will support more weight and will drain much better than fine-grained soils. Soils such as clays and stilts, besides having poor structural and drainage capacities, also have a tendency to expand as they become saturated with ground water and then shrink as they dry. This can cause major problems such as cracking and excessive settling of walks, patios, and footings. If you suspect that the soil on your site has these characteristics,

smart tip

GOOD FOUNDATIONS

BE SURE TO INCLUDE A 4- TO 6-INCH LAYER OF GRAVEL UNDER YOUR PATIO AND WALKWAYS. THE GRAVEL ACTS AS A DRAINAGE SYSTEM THAT KEEPS WATER FROM COLLECTING OR PONDING BENEATH THESE SHALLOW CONSTRUCTIONS.

you should excavate it to a suitable depth and replace it with coarser soil.

Almost every county in the United States has a County Soil Conservation Service, which will provide countywide soil surveys, indicating the predominant soil types in your area. Another source for this information is your local plant nursery, which will have a general knowledge of soil types in your community.

DEALING WITH DRAINAGE

UNLESS YOU HAPPEN TO LIVE on a rock in the middle of the Mojave Desert, you probably already know where the low spots on your site are. You know the locations of those miniature bogs and swamps where the water tends to collect after every good rain. Note and record these places, as well as the existing natural drainage patterns, on your site plan. Here is your opportunity to correct any annoying or destructive drainage problems you may find on your property.

However, the best advice is to identify and work with the natural drainage paths whenever possible. (See "Drainage" on page 34.) These existing paths have generally reached a state of equilibrium with the surrounding terrain. Altering, blocking, or interfering with these natural paths requires expert planning, extra labor, and materials. Re-grading a site can be disastrous if not done properly.

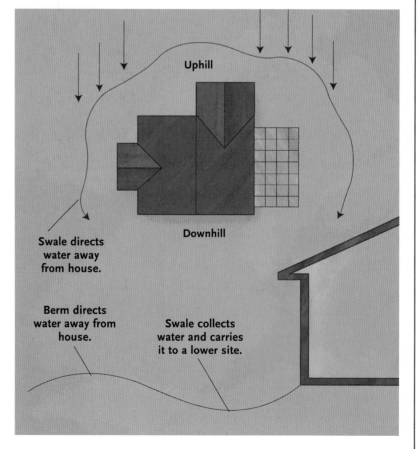

Uphill

Downhill

Swale directs water away from house.

Berm directs water away from house.

Swale collects water and carries it to a lower site.

When planning your landscape design, it's best to consider the natural characteristics of the site, including the soil. On a sloping lot, it's important that the soil is a type that will drain well.

DRAINAGE

Site drainage involves the collection of rainwater and snow runoff, the channeling of this water, and the disposal of the excess water. There are two primary kinds of systems: surface drain systems and subsurface drain systems, such as area drains, catch basins, trench drains, dry wells, and drain tiles. Due to the expense and work involved, use subsurface systems only as a last resort.

Surface drain systems basically consist of shallow drainage ditches, called "swales," and built-up mounds that direct runoff, called "berms." After you have identified where runoff enters your site, decide where to channel it. Generally, it's best to direct it to an existing storm sewer located in the street. Try to channel the water with swales, berms, and retaining walls. If for any reason it is impossible to run storm water to the street system, a substitute location must be chosen (and, no, not in your neighbor's yard). The new drainage pattern should not cause damage to or increase runoff to surrounding properties.

GRADING YOUR SITE

SITE GRADING INVOLVES RESHAPING and recontouring the earth, which is a fancy way of saying "moving a lot of dirt around." Try to work with the existing contours whenever possible to minimize time and expenses. Grading consists of two basic steps: cutting and filling. A cut involves removing dirt (that is, cutting into a hillside), and a fill involves adding dirt to the site's original grade. To avoid having to move excess dirt to or from your property, try to balance the amount of dirt you wish to cut with the amount you wish to fill.

Choosing the Right Slope. Site grading accomplishes two things. The first is functional and involves creating relatively flat areas and walks. The second enhances the aesthetic and sensory qualities of the site. Remember that a completely flat area can be just as undesirable as an excessively steep slope. Water will inevitably collect and remain in a flat area. For this reason, provide a slight slope to play areas, patios, and other areas of use. What you are really trying to do is to find a balance between creating relatively flat areas and avoiding water incursion and ponding. Recommended maximum and minimum slopes for different areas are shown in "Suggested Slopes for Good Drainage" at right. Note that a 0 percent slope is never recommended.

Suggested Slopes for Good Drainage

To determine the percentage of your existing or proposed slopes, simply divide the vertical distance or drop by the horizontal distance (run). For example, a slope that drops 2 feet in 25 feet of run would be equal to an 8 percent slope ($^2/_{25} = 0.08$, or 8 percent).

Here are some recommended slopes for various areas:

	Minimum	Maximum
Walkways, Approaches, and Entrances	0.5%	5%
Patios	1%	2%
Lawn and Play Areas	0.5%	4%
Swales	1%	10%
Grassy Banks		25%
Planted Banks (vines or ground cover)		50%

Hilly locations, above and right, can overcome drainage problems for homes and outdoor living areas with proper excavation of the site and by building suitable walls and berms.

DETERMINING GRADE

TO DETERMINE EXISTING GRADES or set new ones, use this formula: $D = G \times L$

D is the vertical drop in feet; G equals the existing or desired grade as a decimal (2 percent would be 0.02); L equals the horizontal distance in feet.

For example, say you want to slope a 25-foot-long patio a 1-percent grade; the equation would read $0.01 \times 25 = 0.25$ feet (or 3 inches). This means the low end of your patio should be 3 inches below the high end. For existing or desired grades, use $G = D/L$; for lengths, use $L = D/G$

A COMFORTABLE PATIO

A properly designed site can literally extend the comfortable temperature ranges experienced outdoors by several weeks or more. That means a more comfortable patio and backyard beginning earlier in the spring and lasting later into the fall.

Making a Site Cooler or Warmer

Deciduous trees planted to the south and west of your patio will block the summer afternoon sun, which can be uncomfortably hot. Man-made structures that can block the sun include overhead pergolas covered with deciduous vines and strategically placed screen walls.

For cold weather, think of ways to admit direct sunlight while blocking cold winds. For example, a patio that is open to the south but bordered by screens of dense vegetation or solid walls in the other directions will be more comfortable than other parts of the yard. This reflected heat can be as much as 10 degrees warmer than outside these spaces.

Breezes. Strategies for admitting cooling winds in the summer include locating your patio so it is directly in the path of the summer wind. Locate walls and vegetation so that summer winds are directed and channeled into the patio. (See "Location, Location, Location," below.) A deciduous tree, overhead pergola, or screen wall that shades your patio will also prevent sunlight from directly entering the house. The screen wall can also act as a buffer against cold winter winds.

In sunny Southern California, trees provide shade and plantings create privacy on a patio, opposite top.

A walkway, opposite bottom, emphasizes a boundary wall created by the greenery.

LOCATION, LOCATION, LOCATION

IF YOU LIVE IN THE TEMPERATE or cooler regions of the country, the most important overall strategy for locating your patio is to place it to the south, southeast, or southwest side of your house. Here it will receive sun for most of the day, absorb the warming rays, and continue to radiate them back well into the evening. In southern climates, locate your patio to the east or northeast side(s) of the house so that the sun will warm it early in the day when temperatures are relatively cool. In the late afternoon when it's overly warm, a patio located on the east side of a house will be shady. If you live on sloping or uneven terrain, place your patio on high ground because cold, heavy air collects, much like water, and runs down slopes and into valleys and low spots. A patio located in one of these pockets, called a frost pocket, will be much cooler throughout the year.

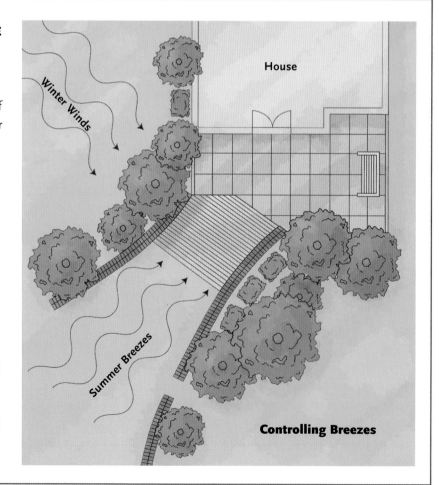

House

Winter Winds

Summer Breezes

Controlling Breezes

Planning Your Site

A USEFUL WALK

Walks connect or link the areas of your site and make them accessible and useful. Beyond solving just the functional aspects of moving around, you can also design walks so that they are pleasant and provide a sense of enjoyment and delight. There are two approaches you can take when placing walks: you can locate certain areas of your site first and then connect them with your walks, or you can lay out your walks, and then locate the other areas.

Staying on the Right Path. Given the chance, people will generally take the shortest, most direct walk from where they are to where they want to go. We've all seen these lines etched into lawn areas where people cut corners, so to speak, to take a more direct route to their destination. In fact, some professional site planners deliberately leave the sidewalks out of the initial construction phase and, a year or so later, go back in and build them when the walks have been worn into the turf.

This may not be a practical approach for you, but it is an argument against laying out strict 90-degree angled walks. Stay flexible, and ask yourself where you really think you'll be walking to get from one place to another on your site.

This site, which is often the setting for breakfast, was selected to take advantage of morning sunlight. Later in the day, and especially during the evening, low shrubs and tall grasses serve as buffers against cool breezes.

DESIGN STRATEGIES FOR WALKS

SHAPE AND SIZE are probably going to be your first considerations. Major walks should be larger and built out of more elaborate or textured materials than minor walks. As for shape, the basic choices are straight, curved, and angled. Straight walks convey a formal sense, but can look a little rigid. Curved walks tend to convey an informal or organic feeling to your site. Curved walks are inherently more flexible and adapt better to sites with slopes and other unusual topography. Don't be afraid to mix different shapes if you feel that's appropriate to your site and needs.

Topography. Topography gets back to one of the main design considerations: always work with the site, not against it. In terms of locating walks, this means avoiding both the steepest areas, which are generally unsafe for most walks, and the lowest spots on your site, where water will collect and damage your walks. On some sites, avoiding slopes and wet spots may be hard. But building through them will also increase your overall costs. The lowest spots on your site may require additional drainage structures, additional fill dirt or gravel to raise the walk above the surrounding grade, or extensive maintenance to keep those portions safe and usable throughout the year.

Safety. Above all, walks must be safe. Features that add to the safety of walks include textured surfaces to improve traction, lighting at critical points, such as steps and landings, and sloped "washes" so that water does not collect or remain on the walkway surface itself. To create a textured surface, use a common straw broom to add a light, medium, or heavy texture to a concrete surface after it has been troweled smooth and just before

Install outdoor lighting along a walkway to ensure everyone's safety.

it finishes setting up. Low-level lighting (5 to 25 foot-candles) at critical points (steps, landings, changes in direction, and entries) makes these places safer at night, and they improve the overall look as well. Easily installed walkway lighting fixtures are readily available at home-improvement stores and can take the form of small ground fixtures, pole-mounted fixtures, or wall-mounted fixtures. Washes are slight tilts of the walk itself to one side or the other so that water will drain off instead of forming puddles.

Accessibility. Accessiblity goes hand in hand with safety. Any walkway that rises or drops more than 6 inches per 10 feet of horizontal run or length is considered a ramp. In northern climates, ramps can be extremely dangerous when they are covered in snow or ice. If you are designing to meet current Americans with Disabilities Act (ADA) standards for wheelchair- or walker-dependent users, the maximum rise permitted for every 12 feet of horizontal run is 1 foot. In addition, current ADA standards require that for every 30 feet of horizontal run or length, a level landing of at least 5 feet must be provided for resting. Also, handrails must be provided on both sides of the ramp no matter how high it is.

TREE AND PLANT GUIDELINES

TREES AND OTHER PLANTS will complement your walk, wall, or patio. Here are a few simple tricks that landscapers and landscape architects use to help them design plantings for a yard. These same tricks can help you.

■ Try to group trees and shrubs into twos and threes. Single plantings appear unnatural and sparse.

■ Limit the overall variety of plants around your site so that there is a sense of unity and order versus randomness and chaos.

■ Use ground covers and grasses as the floors of the site. Bushes, hedges, and shrubs are the outdoor walls. Tree trunks are the columns when defining outdoor spaces, and tree canopies are the outdoor equivalent of ceilings. With these visual images in mind, your task of designing outdoor spaces becomes much easier.

■ Trees and plantings, although obviously natural and organic, can be used in geometric or formal arrangements as well. A well-balanced variety of formal and informal planting arrangements can provide a pleasing contrast and enhance the mood you desire.

■ Be careful not to plant deep-rooted trees next to your house or directly over underground utility lines.

■ Use trees to define and frame your best views and screen or block the undesirable ones.

A curved walk is the perfect complement to the formality of this columned entry, left.

This informal stone path, below, meanders casually toward and through the garden gate.

SITE DESIGN

It's time to put pencil to paper, and design the walk, wall, or patio that's right for your yard. The key to it all is a simple scale drawing of your yard that takes into account the terrain, the house, and the neighborhood.

Take a look at your yard. What size is it? Where is the house? The building department is going to ask you the same questions, and the easiest and most precise answer is a simple map. If you know where the property corners are, you can draw your own. If not, look at the plat map, found at your title company or county tax assessor's office. (A quick search through your house purchase records might also produce a small copy of the plat map.) Depending on the age of your house, you might also be able to obtain a site plan with these dimensions from the builder or from the building department, which typically requires a dimensioned site plan before issuing a building permit. Once you've verified the size and shape of the house and lot, take an inventory of a few other important things.

A largely wooded site originally, the area behind this house was partially cleared to make way for a spacious outdoor living area.

SITE INVENTORY

YOU MAY OWN IT, BUT... there are things besides soil and topography you should also know about your site before you build anything on it.

Utility Easements and Street Rights of Way. You don't want to build on part of the land that's been given to a utility company as an easement. A quick call to your local utility companies can tell you if there are any utility easements running through or alongside your property. Sometimes this information can be found on your title insurance report as well. Depending on your situation, you might also want to check with the local transportation department about the street and alley right-of-way. Often, there are restrictions on what can be constructed within a right of way. Street widening projects could have an adverse affect on your plans.

Utility Lines. While you're talking to the utility companies, find out where the sewer, gas, water, power, cable TV, and telephone lines are. All utility companies have maps that show the approximate location of their underground utilities. This is accurate enough for your site plan. Before you begin actual construction, though, call and have these companies locate their lines and the depths exactly. This service is normally free to all utility customers, and many utility districts have a single toll-free number to call for this service. Check the front of your phone book. Utility companies will come to your house and mark the site (usually with different colors of spray paint) to show exactly where and how deep their respective lines are located. Water and sewer utilities are normally buried quite deep to avoid frost and freezing. Other utilities, however, are often in rather shallow trenches and can easily be cut when digging trenches for a walk or wall.

Zoning. City and county zoning ordinances usually have no effect on site-related improvements. Walks, walls, and patios are normally excluded from front-, side-, and rear-yard setbacks. Only enclosed buildings are required to stay behind these setback lines. On the other hand, it pays to visit the local planning department and verify just how your property is zoned and what effect that could have on your plans.

On an elevated site, this home is positioned to take advantage of a lake view year-round.

Legal Restrictions. Most newer subdivisions will have a set of covenants, codes, and restrictions (CCRs) that can affect the type of materials used and perhaps some other aspects of your project. Your property deed or your title insurance report should have this information. Become familiar with these requirements before designing: this will help you avoid any unpleasant surprises down the road. If you live in an older neighborhood, check with the local planning department to see if any historic district restrictions apply to your site.

Natural Physical Features. Note and record existing trees and vegetation you'll want to save. Be on the lookout for rock outcroppings, shallow layers of bedrock, or extremely rocky soils you'll want to avoid. Note drainage swales, ditches, ponds, streams, and soil types on your site. Perhaps the most important natural feature to observe and record is the topography of your site. This means accurately measuring and locating all the sloping areas, flat areas, high points, ridges, mounds, low points, and valleys. This is important for two reasons: first, it tells you what the drainage patterns are. Second, it provides a basis for working with your site contours during the design process instead of against them.

Man-made Features. Along with the natural features of your site, record any man-made improvements, such as existing fences, walks, retaining walls, curb cuts, utility poles, and fire hydrants, and any other elements that will impact your landscaping plans. Measure and record these items in relation to a fixed reference point, such as the corner of your house, shed, or garage.

Climate Conditions. Unless you live in a warm climate with basically a single season, check with your local weather bureau, airport, or university to find seasonal information for your area. Things to look for include average monthly amounts of rainfall and snowfall, average monthly temperature, typical wind directions for both summer and winter months, and the seasonal sun angles for your location. This kind of information is easy to obtain and can be helpful when you get ready to locate features such as patios or planting beds.

Views and Vistas. No site inventory would be complete without noting the best, and worst, views from the various points. Good views are a special site amenity that should be preserved and, if possible, enhanced through careful planning and design. Technically, a view is an open sweep of landscape such as distant mountains or the seaside, while a vista is a portion of that view, usually with a single element as its focus. As you design your new site plan, make the most of your property's best vistas by opening them up from important locations on your site. Consider how to take visual pleasure in the different seasons. Conversely, use this chance to screen or block unwanted, undesirable views.

Planning Your Site

MAKING A SITE PLAN

NOW THAT YOU'VE SPENT SOME TIME taking inventory of your yard and thinking about what you want to include in your site, you need to organize your thoughts by drawing up a site plan. There's a logical sequence to preparing site plans. In general terms, the drawings proceed from the large elements of the plan and progress toward the smallest details.

Existing Site Plan. The first step is to make a rough sketch of your site, including the house and the shape of the yard. Begin with the existing deed map, site plan, or plat map you gathered earlier. Reproduce it exactly on a large piece of tracing paper with graph lines on it (available at stationery shops or art supply stores). For large landscape projects, draw the entire property: show its overall dimensions, its orientation (relative to north), the location of the house and other buildings, and setback distances and easements from property lines, buildings, and streets. For smaller projects, just draw the affected portion of the property.

The base map should also show your house's floor plan. If you have architect's blueprints of your house, use them to show the location of exterior doors, as well as windows for views. Show the location of other buildings and permanent structures on the property, such as existing walks, walls, fences, detached garages, storage sheds, decks, patios, and the like. Show the location of underground utility lines, pipes, and cables. Draw in the size and location of existing plantings, such as trees, hedges, and shrubs as well as lawn areas, planting beds, and borders. Indicate which trees and shrubs are to be kept and which will need to be removed or relocated during the project.

Rough Layout. Now the fun begins. Attach an overlay of tracing paper to the base map. This is where you should begin sketching and actually placing your outdoor areas. Begin with very loose diagrams as you try out different locations for the walks, walls, and patios on your site. The quicker and looser these early sketches are, the better. This allows you to try out many different ideas, locations, and configurations rapidly and without having to commit to the very first plan layout or idea that you have.

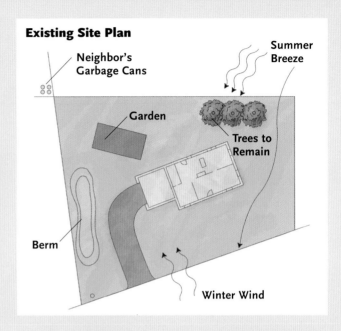

Existing Site Plan

Neighbor's Garbage Cans

Summer Breeze

Garden

Trees to Remain

Berm

Winter Wind

Final Layout. Don't like what you've done? Tear off the overlay and start again. Want to improve on a pretty good design? Add another overlay, and edit your design as you trace it. Keep drawing and improving until you're happy with what you see. Then take a little time to reflect on the design itself. Ask someone familiar with your site to review your design. Oftentimes, designers get so close to and wrapped up in their designs that it is literally hard to see the forest for the trees.

Make sure the design fulfills your intended purpose. If you plan to do a lot of entertaining on your patio, make sure it is large enough to comfortably accommodate the number of guests that you expect will visit at one time. Ask yourself whether the design fits the site, the house, and the surrounding neighborhood. Does the design create a memorable experience for friends and family? Does it have physical or sensory elements that would make the typical visitor want to return? Have you combined walks, walls, and patios in such a way as to create a pleasing atmosphere or mood that will be remembered? Can you can build your design within your budget? We all want the moon, but take a hard look at the estimated costs for what you intend to build.

Make sure your design minimizes maintenance requirements, such as cleaning, sweeping, mowing, water-

Rough Layout

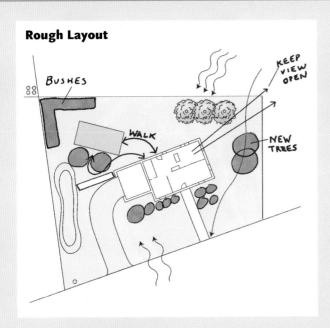

Final Layout

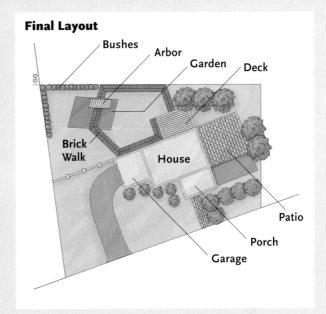

ing, snow removal, painting, or sealing. Some designs look fantastic on paper and then turn out to be real maintenance headaches.

Once you've answered these questions, you may go back and make some final revisions. But when you're happy with what you see, you're ready to start building. Don't forget to take a copy of the final site plan with you when you go to obtain the building permit.

smart tip

DESIGN FOR EVERYONE

IF SOMEONE IN YOUR FAMILY OR AMONG YOUR FRIENDS HAS SPECIAL NEEDS, REVIEW YOUR PLANS— ESPECIALLY WALKWAYS— IN LIGHT OF THIS FACT. HOW EASY WILL IT BE FOR HIM OR HER TO GET AROUND? WILL YOUR FRIEND BE ABLE TO GET TO ALL PARTS OF YOUR SITE OR ONLY CERTAIN AREAS? ARE THE WALKS WIDE ENOUGH TO ACCOMMODATE SOMEONE IN A WHEELCHAIR? COULD YOUR DESIGN ACCOMMODATE RAMPS IN THE FUTURE IF NECESSARY?

walk basics

3

WHEN YOU PLAN A WALK, think of how it will be used and who will use it. Walks must be appropriate in size and materials to accommodate different types of traffic, which can include pedestrians, children on bicycles, people in wheelchairs, people moving materials, and more. In practical terms, walks are just one part of an overall landscape theme, complementing fences, gates, walls, patios, decks, planning areas, and other features. This chapter focuses on design options and requirements for all kinds of walks.

PLAN FOR YOUR NEEDS

Consider size carefully when you're designing a walk. Even a narrow one should be a minimum of 2 feet wide, which enables one person to walk comfortably along it. Garden walks that will bear the traffic of wheelbarrows, seed spreaders, and other wheeled equipment should be at least 3 feet wide. Walks that are 4 feet or wider allow two people to stroll comfortably side by side or pass in opposite directions. Ideally, walks leading to home's front entrance should be 4 feet wide. If you have a wheelchair user in the family, access walks should be at least 5 feet wide.

One of the key decisions you must make when designing a walk is which material to use. Walks can be divided into two basic categories, based on the walk's surface material: hard walks, which are composed of brick or stone; and soft walks, which include those made with wood or loose aggregate.

This newly paved stone walk will receive lots of traffic in the years to come, but it should hold up well and with a minimum amount of maintenance.

HARD WALKS

HARD WALKS CAN BE COMPOSED OF poured concrete or unit masonry materials, such as brick, stone, concrete pavers, and quarry tile. While initial installation may be expensive, hard walks require little maintenance to keep them looking good for many years. Hard materials are preferable in high-traffic areas, such as front walks. Choose your materials carefully. A cobblestone or rough flagstone entry walk may look good, but high heels can get caught between the joints. Avoid surfaces that become slippery in the rain, such as glazed ceramic tile. Unglazed quarry tiles are a safer choice.

Most hard walks must be laid on a firm, well-drained subbase or they tend to buckle, crack, or sink. A subbase consisting of 4 inches of compacted gravel topped by 2 inches of builder's sand (also called torpedo sand) should suffice. The subbase not only provides a solid, well-drained base but also makes it easier to level the paving units. Poorly drained soils or those subject to frost heave, settling, and erosion may require a subbase of 6 to 8 inches of gravel or crushed stone.

In mild climates, large, relatively flat stones more than 1½ inches thick can also be set directly on level, well-tamped soil or recessed into it. Such walks look quite attractive when the joints between the stones are planted with low-growing ground covers, such as Irish moss, dichondra, or woolly thyme.

A paving material, such as paving brick, concrete patio blocks, flagstones, or quarry tile laid over a concrete subbase, makes a durable walk. The concrete—either an existing sidewalk or a new slab—supports the paving material and keeps it from cracking or shifting with freeze-thaw cycles.

WALK DIMENSIONS

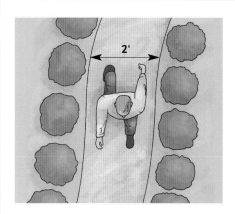

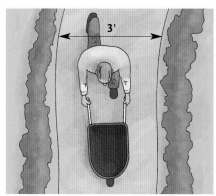

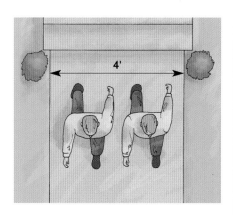

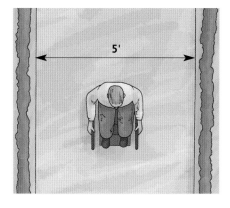

A welcoming brick walk connects the driveway to the terrace in one sweeping curve. It also helps to create a boundary between the wide open spaces of the large yard and the cozy gardens and living areas near the house.

Walk Basics

SOFT WALKS

THE TERM SOFT WALKS refers to walks that consist of wood or any loose aggregate, such as gravel, decorative rock, crushed shells, wood chips, and bark. Often, these materials are used for walks or paths in rustic or informal garden settings or in areas where only occasional foot traffic is expected. The main advantage of soft walks is that they're relatively easy and inexpensive to install and repair. Unlike masonry walks, soft walks aren't affected by unstable soil or frost heave, so you don't need to be as particular about the base you install beneath them. In fact, the base is often nothing more than tamped earth.

Loose materials usually have to be replenished every year, however, because they are kicked into surrounding areas or worked into the soil beneath. As a preventive measure, install a sturdy, raised edging, which can be as attractive as it is practical. The edging will keep the loose paving material from spreading into surrounding areas. In addition, placing landscape fabric on the soil will prevent the paving material from mixing with the earth and deter weed growth.

Soft walks usually work best on flat ground—the aggregate can erode if the walk is built on a slope. Also, keep in mind that most loose aggregates make rougher going for wheeled equipment, such as lawn mowers, wheelbarrows, and wheelchairs. Some materials, such as crushed stone and gravel, are tough on bare feet and hard to navigate in dress shoes.

Wooden Walks. Walks made from lumber are also considered "soft." Naturally decay-resistant woods, such as redwood and cedar, are undeniably beautiful, but they can be expensive. Fortunately, the wide availability of treated lumber has made wood practical and economical for walks and edging. Treated wood that has been rated for ground contact may be installed without worry below ground or on grade.

Wood is also a good material for temporary walks—simply attach top boards to flat 2x4 stringers to create modules of any size. You can relocate or rearrange the modules as your landscape requirements change.

EDGING

Edging is both decorative and functional. Placed along the sides of a walk, edging defines borders and contains the walk's material. All soft walks require raised edging to keep the material in place. Brick and other masonry walks also need edging if they are to be dry-laid on a sand bed. In such cases, the edging not only holds the pavement in place but also serves to contain the bed on which the paving is set. If the walk materials will be mortared in place, edging is more decorative than structural, and its use is optional. If a concentrated load will be placed at the edge, however, you will need to reinforce the edges. If the walk is located where an automobile will drive over it, for example, you should either pour a thickened concrete edge along each side of the walk or install heavy timbers or railroad ties flush with the concrete surface.

A garden path composed of wood chips is a less-austere alternative to gravel or stone. In addition, it has a more natural appearance.

smart tip

PLASTIC EDGE RESTRAINTS

IF YOU'RE INSTALLING A BRICK OR PAVER WALK AND YOU DO NOT WANT A VISIBLE EDGING, YOU CAN USE SPECIAL MOLDED-PLASTIC EDGE RESTRAINTS. SEVERAL TYPES ARE AVAILABLE THAT WILL CONFORM TO STRAIGHT OR CURVED WALKS. TO INSTALL THEM, PLACE THE PLASTIC STRIPS ALONG LAYOUT LINES ON THE GRAVEL SUBBASE. THE EDGING IS HELD IN PLACE WITH 12-INCH SPIKES DRIVEN INTO THE GROUND.

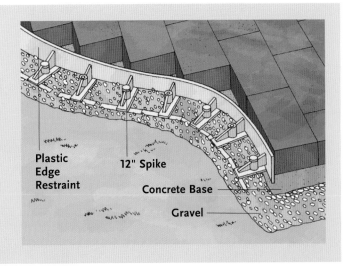

Plastic Edge Restraint

12" Spike

Concrete Base

Gravel

Uniform bricks, above, chosen to match the house facade, create an attractive border for this cut-stone walk, stairs, and landing.

An edging material that contrasts with a walkway, top right and above, defines the lines of the path, helps to keep it neat, and adds another design element.

EDGING MATERIALS

EDGING MATERIALS MAY BE wood, brick, concrete block, stone, or poured concrete, which can match or contrast with the paving material. Plastic edging, which is completely buried after it's installed, is also available. Wood and plastic edging require no forms and are simply anchored to the ground with stakes or spikes. When installing most masonry edging, however, you must set up temporary forms to hold the edging units in a straight line and to act as leveling guides.

In choosing edging materials, decide how you want to install them. Most walk surfaces are slightly higher than the surrounding ground. Edging is usually flush with the pavement or slightly recessed to allow for water runoff. If the walk is on or below grade, however, a raised edging keeps surrounding soil from washing onto the walk and serves to contain plantings. A continuous edging of wood or poured concrete can prevent grass and weeds from spreading from the lawn to the walk.

Wooden Edging. Pressure-treated landscape ties (usually 4x6s or 6x6s) make massive and sturdy edging that is easy to cut and install. They work with all types of paving materials and can serve as forms for poured-concrete walks—simply leave the timbers in place after the concrete is poured. Plan the excavation so that the edging timbers rest on a 4-inch base of gravel or sand, and anchor them in place with rebar spikes.

If landscape ties are too massive for your walk design, you can use pressure-treated 2x6s or 2x8s. Set these boards in the ground at the desired height, and hold them in place with pressure-treated 2x3 stakes. When the walk is complete, backfill over the stakes with topsoil.

Wooden Edging

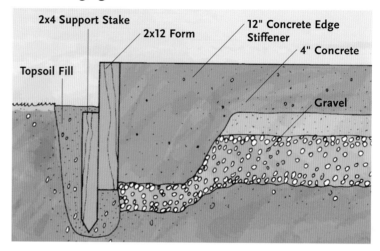

2x4 Support Stake
2x12 Form
12" Concrete Edge Stiffener
4" Concrete
Topsoil Fill
Gravel

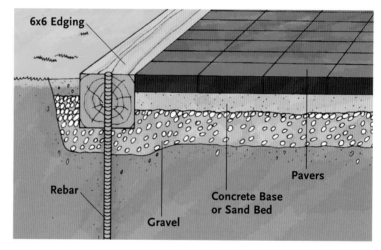

6x6 Edging
Rebar
Gravel
Concrete Base or Sand Bed
Pavers

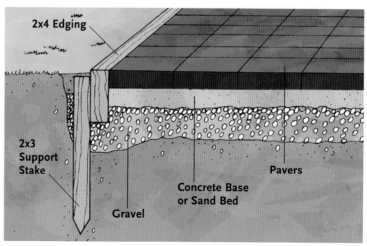

2x4 Edging
2x3 Support Stake
Gravel
Concrete Base or Sand Bed
Pavers

Brick Edging. Bricks make attractive edging that is simple to install in a variety of patterns. It's a good choice for edging curved walks as well. Depending on soil conditions, bricks can be set directly in the ground, or they can be set over a gravel-and-sand subbase. For more stability, you can set the bricks into a poured-concrete footing.

Block Edging. Concrete edging blocks, manufactured to match patio blocks, may be set in a ribbon of concrete along the walk perimeter.

Edging blocks come in straight or curved shapes with various top designs. The blocks typically measure 2 x 5 x 24 inches. This type of edging also may be used by itself as planting-bed borders or in combination with other walk materials.

Stone Edging. Cut stones, cobblestones, and small boulders make good edging for wide walkways. Cut stones, thick flagstones, and cobblestones should be set in a ribbon of concrete to keep them from shifting. Large, irregular boulders can be set in concrete or directly in

the ground. For informal walks, you can dig a small hole for each stone and place it in the ground. This design will not work in more formal areas.

When edging narrow walks, however, you should avoid irregularly shaped stones because they are easily tripped over or kicked out of place. If you're installing a flagstone walk, find out about the availability of thicker border stones that match the type you are using to create the path.

Concrete Edging. Another alternative to edging brick and other masonry-unit walks is to pour a concrete curb. The curb will require formwork, which can be either straight or curved.

A 6- to 8-inch-wide curb that is set 6 to 8 inches in the ground should be adequate for most applications and localities, but check with your building department. Place the concrete on a 4-inch-thick bed of gravel or gravel and sand. Before removing the forms, go over their top edges using an edging tool to make them round.

Stone Edging

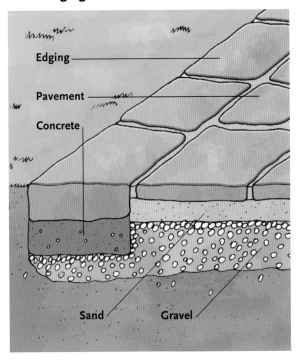

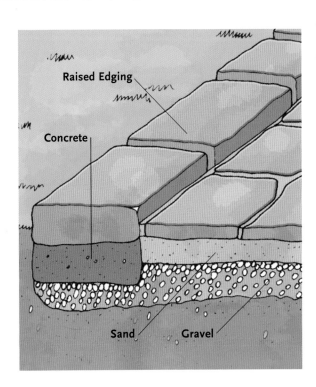

GRADING

The characteristics of the site—terrain, soil conditions, and drainage requirements—as well as the paving material you use determine how to prepare the ground for the walk. Virtually every walk project will require some amount of excavation to create a level surface and to provide a stable base for the paving materials. Installing a walk on a sloped or uneven lot will require extensive cutting and filling to provide a level walking surface. Where the walk runs parallel with a slope, you may need to install low retaining walls on both sides of the walk so that it will be level across its width. If your walk requires extensive grading and excavation, it's best to hire an excavation contractor to do the work.

Changes in Walk Level

On lots with only minor changes in grade or terrain, a hard-surface walk may be able to follow the contour of the land, provided that the walk doesn't become submerged during the rainy season. But for soft walks, the ground must be level, or the aggregate could wash away from high spots and collect in low spots, leaving bare areas. Steeper slopes or grades are usually dealt with by means of steps. If the slope is fairly gentle, you can install long sections of level walkways interspersed with steps. For steeper slopes, flights of stairs connected by landings may be the best solution. To determine how many steps are needed, calculate the total amount of rise between the uphill side of the walk and the downhill side, then divide this measurement by the riser height of each step. (Risers should be no more than 8 inches high.)

This walk runs level with the site, so it probably poses no concerns regarding drainage. However, sometimes a flat site requires some grading to create a slight slope if water collects or puddles on the walk.

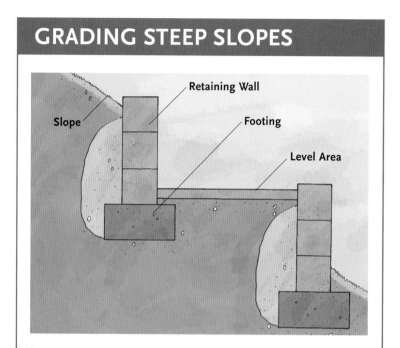

GRADING STEEP SLOPES

Slope

Retaining Wall

Footing

Level Area

DRAINAGE FOR WALKS

DRAINAGE IS USUALLY NOT A MAJOR CONCERN when building a walk. Typically, a building lot is graded so that water runs away from the house, and a walk that runs along grade level presents no problems. In some cases, however, the walk area will have to be graded to provide a slight slope for drainage. If you anticipate drainage problems, sloping the concrete walk ¼ inch per foot along its length will provide adequate drainage in most situations.

In wet soil, you may want to install a perforated drainage pipe in a gravel subbase to assist drainage. If the walk crosses a low area subject to puddling or periodic flooding during the rainy season, loose aggregates, such as gravel or bark, will soon wash away or become mixed with dirt and debris washed in from surrounding areas. In such cases, you should install raised edging and build up the walk materials above the level of the surrounding soil. Don't install walks that cross swales or run across slopes. Such walks can act as dams that impede natural drainage patterns in the yard.

Often, walks made of bricks or concrete pavers are higher in the middle, or crowned, to prevent puddles from gathering on the walk. The crown (measured from the center of the walk to the edge) should be about ⅛ inch per foot. A 4-foot-wide walk, for example, is crowned ¼ inch in the middle. Poured-concrete and flagstone walks are often sloped across their width (about ⅛ inch per foot) to shed water. If a hard walk is next to a garden wall or the house, slope it away from the structure.

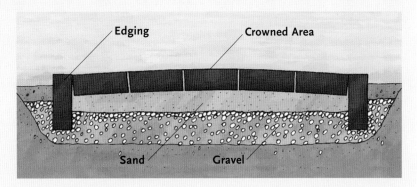

Edging   Crowned Area

Sand   Gravel

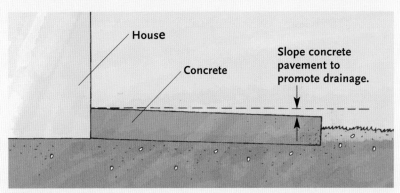

House

Concrete

Slope concrete pavement to promote drainage.

Designed to run in the direction of the site's natural slope, this home's front walk should not have a drainage problem.

soft walks

4

SOFT WALKS ARE MADE OF loose stone, wood, or wood products. They are less expensive and easier to install than hard-surface walks, but they require more maintenance. Because of the variety of materials available, soft walks can take on a number of different looks. Gravel and pebbles come in an array of colors and sizes. Wood walks can be built from loose aggregate, including bark, wood chips, and mulch, or from lumber.

LAYOUT AND PREPARATION

In most cases, wood walks made from boards require a gravel subbase, but stone and wood loose aggregates may be placed directly on the ground. Usually, edging will be required to contain loose aggregate. Even with edging, however, foot traffic will disperse loose aggregate into the surrounding area, and if the area is a lawn, a lawnmower blade can turn the aggregate into dangerous projectiles. On the other hand, both stone and wood aggregates will conform to any shape walk, which makes these materials highly desirable for surfacing meandering garden paths.

Lumber walks can take many shapes and can be raised above grade level to bridge rough terrain or low areas. For high-traffic areas, a lumber walk offers the advantages of easy installation and repair and can unify other wood elements, such as a deck or siding, with the landscape.

STONE AGGREGATE

In general, stone aggregate is a good choice for walks that receive light traffic. Because it dries quickly and drains efficiently, crushed stone is a good choice for garden paths. To cover 100 square feet of walkway with a 2-inch layer of stone, you will need about ⅔ cubic yard of material.

As for its disadvantages, stone must be replenished, raked, and tamped periodically. When compared with a hard walk surface, pushing a wheelbarrow over loose stone requires more effort, and walking in dress shoes or bare feet can be difficult, if not painful.

Types of Stone

Stones used for soft walks may be classified by their texture, either smooth or rough. Generally, rough stones make a tighter, more compact walk than do smooth stones. Both textures are available in many colors and sizes, but choose carefully. Pick a color that won't overwhelm the landscape—blue rocks that look attractive in the bag may end up as an electric blue river in your yard. Also, light-color stones stain easily, so they won't be appropriate for a high-traffic path.

Although loose aggregate ranges from ¼-inch pebbles to 3-inch stones, the best sizes are between ¾ and 1½ inches. Medium-size stones stay in place better than small pebbles, and they compact better and are more comfortable to walk on than large stones.

Gravel and Crushed Stone. You can buy gravel or crushed stone in uniform sizes or in random sizes, called unscreened gravel. Because gravel is jagged, it compacts well, but it's also uncomfortable to walk on barefoot. Typically blue-gray in color, gravel is also commonly available as reddish brown redrock, white dolomite, and multicolor decomposed granite.

Smooth Stone. River stone is smooth, making it more comfortable to walk on barefoot but less likely to stay compacted. River stone usually consists of white, tan, and gray rocks, which have been rounded smooth either naturally or by machine. Like gravel, river stone is sold in a variety of sizes by the bag or by the yard at stone yards and garden centers.

The winding crushed-stone walkway opposite adds another texture and blends organically into an informal landscape. This is a good choice for low-traffic areas.

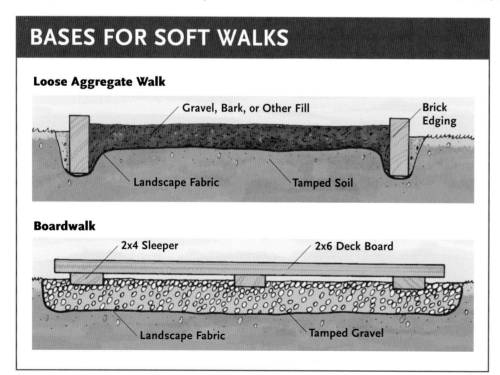

BASES FOR SOFT WALKS

Loose Aggregate Walk

Gravel, Bark, or Other Fill

Brick Edging

Landscape Fabric

Tamped Soil

Boardwalk

2x4 Sleeper

2x6 Deck Board

Landscape Fabric

Tamped Gravel

Soft Walks

PLOTTING CURVES

CURVED WALKS CAN BE LAID OUT in a freeform design or by "drawing" a series of arcs on the ground with a giant compass, made from a rope, a stake, and a sharp stick. Tie one end of the rope to the stake and drive it into the ground. Mark the desired radius on the rope, and tie the stick at the mark. Swing the rope and stick around the stake, scratching the arc on the ground. Adjust the length of the rope to lay out the other side of the walk.

Lay out an irregular curve using a rope or garden hose. Outline one side of the curve with the rope or hose. Cut a series of sticks the width of the walk, and place them at regular intervals, as shown. Outline the other side of the curve with a second rope or hose. Then sprinkle flour or sand to mark the curves. Dig a trench deep enough to accommodate a curved form (which can be made from bending thin plywood) or a permanent edging material, such as bricks.

WOOD AGGREGATE

Loose wood-aggregate walks are simpler and less expensive to install than lumber walks, but they won't last nearly as long. Bark, wood chips, and mulch make a soft, springy walkway that you can kneel on comfortably when gardening. Like stone, wood aggregates are recommended for light-traffic areas and are difficult to negotiate with wheeled equipment or in high heels. Most kinds of wood aggregate will last only a few years before decomposing. Bark and redwood chips will last longer, but they are expensive. Wood aggregate tends to hold moisture, and it will wash away in a heavy rain, leaving bare spots. Avoid using it in areas subject to flooding or with poor drainage. Even under good circumstances, wood aggregate requires regular raking and replenishing. To cover 100 square feet of walkway with a 2-inch layer of wood aggregate, you will initially need about $2/3$ cubic yard of the material.

Bark Chips. Sold by the bag, bark chips come in a variety of sizes, from $1/4$ to 3 inches. Two common types, firbark and tanbark, have a dark color and a rustic texture that complement a natural landscape. Generally, bark lasts longer but is more expensive than wood chips.

Wood Chips. Typically light in color, wood chips are the by-product of milling or tree-clearing operations. Wood chips sold by the bag are purer than those sold by the yard, which often contain leaves, twigs, and bark, but the bagged form is also more expensive. Landscapers and utility companies sometimes sell wood chips at reasonable prices by the truckload.

Mulch. Mulch refers to a variety of organic materials cut to small sizes, such as ground bark, sawdust, conifer needles, and shredded roots. Among all loose aggregates, mulch offers the most comfortable walking surface.

LOOSE-AGGREGATE WALK (STONE OR WOOD)

In circumstances where drainage is not a problem, soft walk materials can be placed in a shallow excavation. It's not necessary to build up a gravel subbase. Simply tamp the soil at the bottom of the excavation.

Begin by laying out the walk using stakes and string. Drive two 1x2 stakes at each end of the walk, positioned to indicate the edges of the walk. Then attach string to the stakes to mark the finished height of the edging.

TOOLS & MATERIALS

▐ Spade (for removing sod) ▐ Rake or hoe
▐ Hand or mechanical tamper
▐ Rubber mallet ▐ Stakes and string
▐ Gravel or wood aggregate
▐ Landscape fabric ▐ Bricks for edging

1 Some type of continuous edging is usually needed to hold loose aggregates in place. After excavating and leveling the walkway bed, install wood stakes and run string lines to serve as a guide for the edging. Then dig narrow trenches on each side of the walkway deep enough for the brick, stone, cobblestone, or other edging of your choice.

2 Spread landscape fabric over the length and width of the walkway to discourage weed growth. A fabric base also prevents loose aggregates from disappearing into the soil and reduces the need to replenish the aggregates over time. Overlap the fabric where sections meet, and tuck the fabric into the trenches on both sides of the walkway. Backfill the edging with compacted soil.

3 Bed the edging into the trenches by tapping with a wood or rubber mallet (inset). The trenches should be deep enough so that the top of the edging material meets the string. Fill the walkway with aggregate to about half the depth of the edging; then tamp the material well. Repeat with another layer of aggregate to just below the top of the edging.

LUMBER WALKS

Compared with most hard walk materials, such as concrete and brick, lumber is easy to cut and install. It's less expensive than most paving materials, and depending on the type of lumber you choose, a wood walk may last as long as a hard walk. To build a lumber walk, all you need are a few basic layout and carpentry tools, a shovel, a rake, and a wheelbarrow. If you're laying the walk on or below grade, you should provide a level, well-drained base of gravel.

Some lumber species, notably redwood, cypress, and cedar, are naturally resistant to decay and can be used to construct wood walks, albeit expensive ones. A more economical approach is to use pressure-treated lumber. You can install a durable, long-lasting treated-wood walk in, on, or above the ground. Building an aboveground walk is an excellent way to avoid altering existing drainage patterns or to create a level walking surface across uneven or rocky terrain with a minimum of excavation.

Treated Lumber

Treated wood comes in a variety of dimensional sizes, from one-by boards to large landscape timbers and poles. All treated wood is rated according to usage. Lumber rated for ground contact, designated 0.41 (meaning it has a preservative retention of 0.41 pound per cubic foot), is recommended for all walk applications. Preservative doesn't completely penetrate into the center of the board, so you should apply wood preservative to the cut ends. If your design calls for large timbers, use treated landscape ties. Treated timbers are better for walking on than real railroad ties, which are splintery and have a toxic, oily creosote coating.

Untreated Lumber

Naturally decay-resistant woods, such as redwood and cedar, are often used in outdoor projects for appearance's sake. Such woods are recommended for aboveground use only, where they may last 10 years or more, depending on climate and maintenance. Finishing such wood species with paint, stain, or preservative will prolong the life span. Other species, such as pine and fir, have little resistance to decay and are not recommended for walks even if finished.

Wood Rounds and Blocks. In some parts of North America (typically in the West), redwood and cedar rounds are used as "stepping stones." Rounds are sections of log about 3 to 6 inches thick and 12 to 30 inches in diameter, with or without the bark attached. Laid directly on level, well-drained soil or on a compacted-sand base, the rounds

SUBSURFACE DRAINAGE

IF YOU ARE BUILDING A WALK in an area that is subject to flooding dig the walk an extra 6 inches deep and lay a 4-inch perforated drainpipe down the middle. Dig the middle of the excavation a few inches deeper than along the sides to create a sloping bottom.

Spread and tamp a 2-inch layer of gravel (crushed limestone works best) on the bottom. Set the perforated pipe in the middle of the excavation with the perforations down. Continue filling until you can set edging on the fill and have it protrude about 2 inches above grade. If you are setting brick edging, lean the bricks against the sides of the excavation. If the soil will not hold a vertical edge, prop the bricks against wood forms. Add stone to cover the pipe, but leave enough room for a 2-inch layer of walk material. Place a layer of landscape fabric on the crushed gravel; then spread the surface material until it comes within about ¾ inch of the top of the edging.

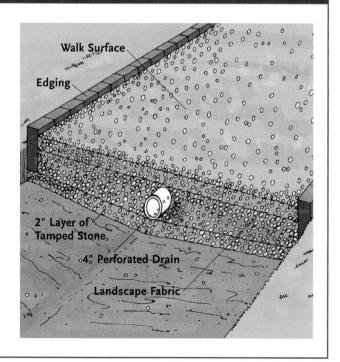

Walk Surface

Edging

2" Layer of Tamped Stone

4" Perforated Drain

Landscape Fabric

LUMBER WALK OPTIONS

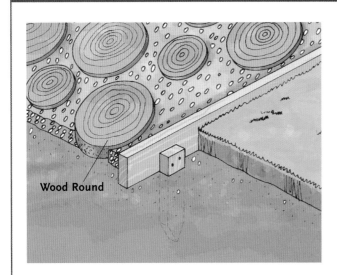

Wood Round

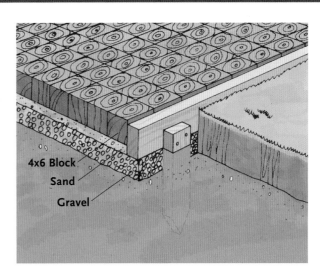

4x6 Block
Sand
Gravel

Another type of walkway can be created with wood boards. (See page 68.)

last about five years before they begin to decay. (Simulated wood rounds, which are formed from concrete, are available at stone yards and patio suppliers and will last much longer.) Plant the spaces between rounds with a ground cover that can withstand light foot traffic. Such plants include Irish moss, lippia, sandwort, and yerba linda. You can also recess the rounds into a soft walk made from a loose aggregate, such as gravel or bark chips. The rounds should be about ½ inch higher than the surrounding loose aggregate so that it won't wash over the rounds.

If wood rounds aren't available in your area and you like exposed end-grain, you can set short timber blocks (either redwood or pressure-treated lumber) vertically in a sand bed. The procedure is similar to that for setting bricks in sand. (See "Laying the Walk" page 88.) Cut the blocks—4x6s or larger timbers—into 3- or 4-inch lengths. Lay enough blocks to calculate the width of the walk. Excavate the walk area; add a gravel-and-sand base; and install the edging before setting the blocks. To avoid drainage problems, set the edging so it will be flush with, or below, the walk surface. Put the blocks end-grain up, and butt them together. Sweep fine sand into the joints.

After setting rounds or timber blocks, brush on a good water sealer or a wood preservative to help prevent checking and cracking. Soaking the blocks or rounds in a wood preservative before installation will extend their life considerably, although the treatment is fairly expensive. Because many wood preservatives are toxic, follow all precautions listed on the label.

Crushed stone pathways meander through this lush, almost wild garden. The reddish brown color of the stone blends with the twig arbors to provide cohesion for the natural-looking design.

Boardwalks

You can build a simple wooden boardwalk by nailing two-by crosspieces to wood sleepers laid either in or on top of a flat, well-drained base of gravel. Make the sleepers from treated wood rated for ground contact. The deck boards can be treated wood or a decay-resistant species. Support walks more than 3 feet wide with a third sleeper running down the center of the walk. For wider walks, space sleepers no more than 3 feet apart.

The walk surface should be at least 1½ inches above grade. To keep washed soil and trash from accumulating underneath the raised walk, attach a two-by header that touches the ground at each end.

The decking can be 2x4s, 2x6s, 2x8s, or wider boards, or a combination of widths. The plank walk described below uses 2x4 sleepers laid flat on top of a gravel sub-base. The walk surface is 2x8 deck boards. The boardwalk at right uses wide two-by sleepers and 2x4 decking.

PLANK WALKS

A PLANK WALK is constructed with 2x8 or wider deck boards that run along the length of the walk and are supported by 2x4 cleats laid across the excavation. Cut the cleats to the exact walk width, and set them every 3 feet directly on a gravel base. Lay the first plank over the cleats, aligned with the layout line; when the end of a cleat is flush with the edge of the plank, fasten the two together. Make sure joints between planks occur over cleats. Use a framing square to keep the cleats perpendicular to the planks. For a finished look and extra support, attach 2x4 or 2x6 edge strips around the perimeter.

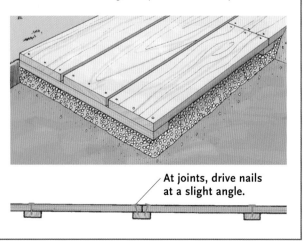

At joints, drive nails at a slight angle.

BUILDING A BOARDWALK

project

At each end of the walk, drive two 1x2 stakes at least 2 feet into the ground to indicate the edges of the walk, and stretch strings between them. Double-check to make sure that the strings are the same distance apart at both ends. If the walk leads straight to an entry, make sure the lines are perpendicular to it by using the 3-4-5 triangulation method, explained in "Using the 3-4-5 Method," page 168.

TOOLS & MATERIALS
- Spade or shovel ▮ Rake or hoe
- Hand or mechanical tamper
- Drill driver ▮ Router
- Round-over bit ▮ Tape measure
- Stakes and strings ▮ Gravel
- Landscape fabric ▮ Lumber for walk
- Treated lumber for sleepers

3 Install the sleepers, using your layout string lines as a guide. Measure and position each two-by board an equal distance in from the string, and use stakes to secure the boards in place. Before attaching the boards to the stakes with nails or decking screws, adjust them to the desired height of the walkway less the thickness of the deck boards.

1 Dig the trench at least 4 in. deep and 8 to 12 in. wider than the walk. Place stakes outside the trench, and use string to mark the excavation width and for laying out your sleepers later. You can build this walk to be level with the grade or slightly above it by adjusting the depth of the trench and gravel base and using appropriately sized sleepers.

2 Lay landscape fabric over the soil, covering the length and width of the trench and overlapping the fabric by several inches where sections meet. To allow for a layer of gravel 4 in. deep at minimum, plus the height of the two-by sleepers, this trench was dug to an 8-in. depth. Add the gravel, rake it level, then firmly tamp as needed.

4 Use 3-in.-long, weather-resistant decking screws to attach the deck boards to the sleepers. Predrill pilot holes if the fasteners are installed close to the board ends. You can use 2x4s, as shown, or 2x6 boards according to the look you want. Be sure to leave space between each of the boards to allow for wood expansion and to let water drain.

5 For a finished look, use a router equipped with a round-over bit to smooth the deck board ends. After the woodwork is completed, backfill all around the walkway with gravel up to the finished grade or to the tops of the sleepers. To extend the life of the boardwalk, use a roller to apply a weather-sealing finish every two to three years.

dry-laid walks 5

DRY-LAID WALKS are among the simplest and most organic types of garden paths you can build, but they are also extremely durable when properly constructed. Essentially, dry-laid walks are made by bedding paving materials on a base of sand and gravel, then filling the joints with soil, sand, or dry mortar. Over time, these natural-looking walks blend into and become an integral part of the landscape, appearing as though they had always been there.

SETTING HARD WALKS

This chapter and the next concern hard walks, made of unit paving materials—brick, concrete pavers, and stone. There are two ways to set these walks: you can dry-lay them or set them in wet mortar. This chapter discusses dry-laid walks, in which paving materials are laid on a bed of tamped sand over gravel. The next discusses laying paving material, in mortar on top of a concrete bed.

Flexible Paving. For dry-laid walks, the joints between paving materials are filled with sand, topsoil, or dry mortar. The width of the joints will help you determine which joint-filling material to use. Paving materials that can be laid closely together, such as bricks and interlocking pavers, are usually set with sand between the joints. In this type of construction, called flexible paving, fine mason's sand is swept into the joints, creating a stable and durable walk, even in climates subject to some frost heave. It's

easy to replace damaged paving materials, fill sunken portions of the walk, or remove sections of the walk to get to buried utility lines or pipes. However, the sand must be replenished annually, and sometimes more frequently.

Wide Joints. Joints between irregularly shaped paving materials, such as flagstones and rubble, are too wide to hold onto sand, so these paving materials have topsoil or mortar joints. If you live in an area where frost heave is not a problem, you can make a simple and attractive walk by setting concrete stepping stones, flagstones (2 inches or thicker), or fieldstones directly on compacted soil. Pack the joints with topsoil. To prevent weed growth, plant the crevices with grass or a low-growing ground cover. Mortared joints make for a smoother, more formal walk than topsoil joints, but they are subject to cracking in a dry-laid walk.

Irregularly shaped stones create a casual, natural-looking walkway, opposite. Although random shapes and sizes are fine for this type of installation, the stones should be the same thickness.

Large paving stones, right, create an informal walk, as well, but they offer a more uniform appearance than random-size stones.

TOOLS YOU WILL NEED

The tools you will need for installing a dry-laid walk will depend on the walk material, but some tools will be used for all walks. For example, the job of compacting the soil and subbase can be done with a hand tamper; however, renting a power tamper is recommended. Power tampers compact soil, gravel, and sand better, faster, and with less effort than tamping by hand.

Screed Board. You can make a screed board to smooth the sand bed. The screed board is a section of 1x6, the ends of which are notched to fit loosely inside the walk borders or edgings. Because the notched ends usually ride on top of the edgings, the notch depth equals the thickness of the paving material. If you're laying dimensional paving materials, such as brick or dressed stone, cut the screed board so that the bottom edge is arched the proper amount to create a crowned walk. When setting irregular paving materials, such as flagstones and rubble, the board is straight because the walk is pitched sideways to shed water.

USING A SCREED BOARD

Notch depth equals pavement thickness.

Curved bottom creates walk surface that drains easily.

Screed

2x3 Stake   4"–6" Gravel   2" Builder's Sand

MATERIAL SELECTIONS

Paving materials that can be laid in a sand bed over a gravel subbase include brick, stone, adobe, concrete patio blocks, and interlocking pavers. Among these choices, some materials are cut to more precise sizes and shapes than others; some materials are better suited to particular climates. Otherwise, walk-construction techniques and required substrates are similar for all of the common paving materials. Exceptions are noted under each heading below. As with any masonry project, check local building codes for specific requirements and accepted practices in your area.

smart tip

GETTING CLEAN CUTS

A BRICK SPLITTER PRODUCES CLEANER AND MORE PRECISE CUTS THAN YOU CAN ACHIEVE WITH A HAMMER AND CHISEL. YOU CAN RENT THEM FROM A TOOL RENTAL OUTLET. ANOTHER OPTION IS A CIRCULAR SAW EQUIPPED WITH A MASONRY BLADE.

BRICK

BRICKS PROVIDE A BEAUTIFUL walk surface that will last for many years, provided that you choose the right kind of brick. That's a formidable task, considering that bricks come in a bewildering array of sizes, colors, and textures, not all of which are suitable for walks. Some bricks are designed for interior applications and won't hold up under wet or freezing conditions; some have smooth or glazed surfaces that can make for a dangerously slippery walk when wet. The ideal brick is hard and dense and has a slightly rough surface to provide good traction in wet weather. Paving brick is designed especially for walks and patios and meets these criteria. The next best choice is face brick, followed by concrete brick.

Paving Brick. Designed especially for ground contact, paving brick is sealed, so it has a high resistance to abrasion and moisture penetration. Most paving bricks are cut to uniform dimensions, so they can be set with perfectly aligned, mortarless joints. You can also get pavers that are sized to work with mortar joints. Some paving bricks, called repress pavers, have chamfered or rounded edges on one or both faces. Repress pavers are preferred in some climates because the chamfered edges facilitate water runoff and are less likely to chip if struck by a snow shovel.

Concrete Brick. If you live in a mild climate and your walk will receive only light traffic, you can save money by using concrete brick. Concrete bricks are not quite as durable as pavers, and their colors, sizes, and textures are often limited. A typical concrete brick measures $2\frac{1}{4}$ x $3\frac{5}{8}$ x $7\frac{5}{8}$ inches. Because this is a manufactured product, the size and coloring are usually very consistent. Unfortunately, the pigments used to color the concrete sometimes fade. As with concrete blocks and pavers, the bricks have a slightly rough, pitted surface.

Durability. Most clay bricks are manufactured to withstand the weather. The most expensive grade, SX paving bricks, will withstand severe weathering, such as freeze-thaw conditions in cold climates and are recommended for outdoor walks and patios. MX paving bricks will withstand moderate weather conditions, including rain and mild frost. Before you start your project, consult your local building department for information on the brick types that are suitable for your particular project. Bricks are also rated for hardness. The hardest, Type I, is the most expensive, but it is rarely used in residential applications. Type II is suitable for residential driveways and entry walks, and Type III is adequate for low-traffic garden walks and patios.

Estimating Bricks. Pavers designed to be used with mortar joints are usually referred to by their nominal size—the actual size plus the width of a mortar joint. Pavers designed for swept-sand joints usually have spacer nubs that leave space for the sand. Whether or not you are using joints, it will take an average of 4.5 bricks to cover a square foot. For example, a 12-foot-by-20-foot patio is 240 square feet. Multiply 240 x 4.5 bricks to find you need 1,080 bricks. Order 5 to 10 percent extra to allow for miscuts, breakage, and future repairs.

Certain brick patterns, such as herringbone and basket weave, require a brick type with a length that is exactly twice its width if the bricks will be set without mortar joints. A standard modular brick works well for these patterns—it has a nominal size of $2\frac{2}{3}$ inches thick, 4 inches wide, and 8 inches long.

Split pavers are half the thickness of a standard brick and are useful when headroom is limited, such as in an enclosed porch. Soap bricks are half the width of a standard brick. Soaps are sometimes used as border bricks for walks or to create special patterns.

Cutting Bricks. If your walk requires a few cut bricks, you can cut them with a brick chisel, or brickset, and small sledgehammer. To cut a brick with a chisel, first mark the cut line with a piece of chalk or grease pencil. With a hammer and brickset, tap all four sides of the brick to score it along the cut line; then center the brickset over the line and strike the chisel sharply. You may have to strike the brickset a few times.

This three-brick weave, above, is a variation on a traditional basket-weave pattern.

You can use mason's sand to fill the joints between these bricks, left, which are of a consistent size.

BRICK PATTERNS

BRICKS REQUIRE CAREFUL LAYOUT to avoid misaligned joints or partial bricks along the edges of the walk. Before you lay the bricks, do a dry run to spot any potential layout problems.

Jack-on-Jack. Also called a stack bond, this pattern is the simplest to lay and the least interesting. Starting at one end of the walk, place a single brick in one corner, then place remaining bricks in stair-step fashion, in the sequence shown. If possible, plan the walk width to avoid cut bricks. If you can't do this, cut the bricks you'll need to the same size, all at once with a masonry saw. Place cut bricks along the least conspicuous edge of the walk, such as against a building or overhanging plant border.

Running Bond. This is the most popular brick pattern and is easy to lay out. Also, the pattern visually minimizes any minor variations in brick sizes. Place the first course of bricks end to end across the walk. Start the second course with a half brick, followed by whole bricks placed end to end so that joints fall midway between bricks as shown.

Herringbone. This pattern looks best on wide walks. On walks 3 feet wide or less, the pattern may appear confusing. As with the running-bond design, a herringbone pattern requires partial bricks along the walk edges and ends, which are best cut in advance on a masonry saw. Starting at one corner, place full bricks in a step pattern, using half bricks to fill in along the edges. Use a framing square to align bricks meeting at right angles.

Weaves. Basket-weave designs look best when you use modular bricks on which the nominal width is exactly half the length. To make a simple two-brick basket weave, lay two bricks side by side to form a square in one corner of the walk. Working across the walk, lay a second square of two bricks at right angles to the first. Alternate the direction of each square until you reach the other

POPULAR BRICK PATTERNS

Jack-on-Jack

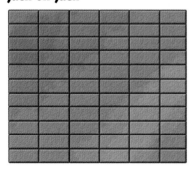

Running Bond

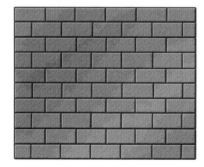

Herringbone

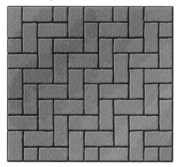

side of the walk. Install the second course by laying two bricks at right angles to the square above it. Continue in this manner to create the pattern shown. Start the half-basket weave as shown, beginning the second course with bats, a brick that is cut in half lengthwise.

The ladder weave combines the weave patterns with the Jack-on-Jack pattern.

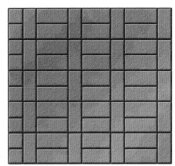

A jack-on-jack pattern is easy to create and easy on the eye, especially on a curved walk, opposite.

Herringbone pattern, left, is set on an angle, adding more interest to the design.

A running-bond pattern, above, staggers the joints, and is always a popular choice.

Basket Weave

Half-Basket Weave

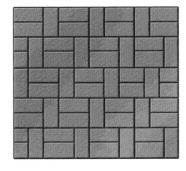

Ladder Weave

smart tip

POWER TAMPING

FOR LARGE PROJECTS, DO YOUR ARMS AND SHOULDERS A FAVOR BY RENTING A VIBRATING TAMPER. YOU CAN USE IT TO SMOOTH OUT GRAVEL AND TO MAKE SURE THE PAVING MATERIAL IS SET FIRMLY.

ADOBE BLOCKS

WITH ITS EARTHY TAN COLOR characteristic of Southwestern and early California architecture, adobe lends a warm, natural feel to the garden. Because traditional adobe is not waterproof, it's used mostly in warm, arid climates. Modern adobe paving blocks, however, are nearly as waterproof as clay bricks. Adobe paving blocks come in a variety of square and rectangular sizes.

Consider using small, brick-size units for walks; large blocks may be out of scale in the landscape. Most adobe block is produced in the Southwest and California, where it is inexpensive compared with standard clay brick. Elsewhere, shipping costs make adobe more expensive.

Installation. Lay adobe on a gravel-and-sand bed, as you would brick. (Follow the instructions in "Laying the Walk," page 88.) The bed should be smooth and pitched slightly across its width to shed water. Set the bricks with wide (¾- to 1-inch) joints to compensate for the irregularity of the edges and to provide sufficient drainage. Pack the joints with sand or well-draining soil. Do not use mortar, which can stain the adobe. Jack-on-Jack and running bond are two popular patterns.

STONE

NATURAL STONE WALKS lend a sense of permanence to the landscape and blend with almost any decor. Stone comes in a variety of colors, shapes, and sizes. The most common types used for walks and patios are split along natural fissure lines to produce a slender, flat stone. Such stones include slate, quartzite, and sandstone. These and many other types of split, or "cleft," stones are available as flagstones and dimensioned paving stones, but you'll usually be limited to what's available in your area.

Ashlar. Ashlar is cut to square or rectangular shapes either in random or uniform sizes to present a more formal appearance. Typically, such stones are laid in a coursed pattern.

Flagstone. Flagstones—usually slate, limestone, or sandstone slabs—come in random shapes and sizes and are fitted together like a jigsaw puzzle in a random pattern. Generally, flagstones are less expensive than ashlar.

Fieldstone. As their name implies, fieldstones are rocks collected from fields, dry creek bottoms, and similar sources. Most fieldstones have a fairly smooth, weathered surface, but their irregular shape makes them difficult to lay in walks. If you have access to a free source of stone (and a means of transporting it to the building site), pick relatively thin, flat stones with smooth surfaces.

Rubble. Rubble is usually the least expensive stone you can buy at rock yards and patio suppliers. It consists of irregularly shaped stones, usually with sharper edges than fieldstone. Rubble may have been blasted from construction sites, or it may be broken pieces left over from cutting quarried stones. At construction sites, rubble is sometimes free for the hauling. Depending on the type, size, and shape of the stones (and their cost), it may or may not be worth your time and energy to haul them home and try to set them into a walk. Consider your walk requirements carefully before choosing rubble or fieldstone.

Installation Tips

Stones for dry-laid walks should be at least 1½ inches thick, as thinner stones may break. With stones of consistent thickness, the sand bed is usually 2 inches thick. Stones of varying thickness should be laid on a thicker sand bed. Remove sand as necessary to create a level walk surface. Along walk edges, use larger stones, which aren't so easily dislodged.

Stonework is backbreaking work, so you should not try to do too much in one day. Also, it's a good idea to enlist the aid of a strong helper. Even modest-size paving stones can weigh 50 pounds or more.

Estimating Amounts. Quarries and patio suppliers sell natural stone either by the ton or by the cubic yard. Because of the spaces between stones and thickness variations, stones sold by weight or by volume may not cover what they are slated to cover. You'll need to rely on the experience of the supplier to calculate your needs. Generally, it's best to order 20 to 25 percent more than you think you need to allow for cutting and breakage. Some suppliers will let you return any unused stones. You can also use any extras in other parts of the yard for stepping stones or plant borders.

Slate flagstones can sit directly on the ground. But be careful, they can be slippery when wet, so you may want to reserve them for an out-of-the-way path.

A walkway made of cut stone is a harmonious choice for this rustic lakeside retreat. For this type of installation, choose large stones that will not become dislodged easily.

INTERLOCKING PAVERS

INTERLOCKING PAVERS are modular concrete units manufactured to fit in a tight pattern. Available in a variety of sizes and shapes, most pavers are 2⅜ to 2½ inches thick, about the same as a standard brick. One type, called a grass paver, has an open-grid shape for planting grass or other ground cover. Grass pavers provide a durable, natural-looking walk surface, and the turf itself helps hold the pavers in place.

For all pavers, check manufacturer's literature for coverage estimates, and buy a few extra for replacement purposes.

Installation. Interlocking pavers are usually butted together and finished with swept-sand joints. Some pavers have small tabs on one side and one end to ensure consistent joint spacing. Laying pavers is much the same job as laying bricks on a sand bed, but check the manufacturer's instructions. (See "Laying the Walk," page 88.) Where soil conditions and climate permit, pavers may be laid directly on well-tamped soil. Depending on the shape of the paver, you may end up with voids or chinks along the edges of the walk. Some manufacturers make special edging pieces to fill the chinks and create a straight edge. Otherwise, you'll have to cut the pavers or fill the voids with mortar to make straight edges.

Interlocking pavers can mimic the look of brick, stone, or tile and let you create all kinds of designs.

CONCRETE PATIO BLOCKS

CONCRETE PATIO BLOCKS are thinner (usually only 1 inch thick) and less expensive than concrete bricks and interlocking pavers. Patio blocks come in a variety of shapes and colors; the standard size is a 1-foot square that is 1 inch thick. The surface texture is similar to that of concrete building blocks used in foundations, although exposed aggregate surfaces are also common and much more attractive.

As with all molded concrete products, there is little size variation in a given run of concrete patio blocks, and their nominal size is the same as their actual size. Therefore, calculating the number of blocks you need is simply a matter of dividing the total walk area by the area of a single unit. Order 10 percent extra, however, because concrete patio blocks are prone to accidental breakage and don't always split cleanly when you cut them.

Installation. Patio blocks should be set on a highly compacted and well-drained sand-over-gravel base, but you should expect some shifting, sinking, and even breakage due to stress or severe weather conditions. Because concrete patio blocks are only 1 inch thick, there's less area for sand to create an interlocking joint than with concrete bricks or interlocking pavers. To provide a better interlock between the patio blocks, space them ½ inch apart and mix the jointing sand with portland cement in a 1:1 ratio. Sweep the dry mixture into the joints; pack it with a thin wood tamper; then wet it and let it dry for two or three days before using the walk.

Large concrete blocks, below, that sit directly on the soil here look modern in a super-size basket-weave pattern.

These patio pavers have been set in a jack-on-jack pattern, below right. The light-color ones used as an inset add a lot of style to a simple design.

Natural "grout" in between these rough-cut slate tiles pop in contrast to the earthy-color stone. If you like this look, you'll have to remember to water and trim the planting or grass regularly to keep it looking healthy and neat.

SETTING STONE DIRECTLY ON THE GROUND

Mostly because it is impractical to construct a sand base for thick, irregularly shaped stones, they may be set directly in stable, well-drained soil that isn't subject to frost heave. These walks have topsoil joints, so they are not as formal or as smooth as walks with sand or mortar joints.

Possible Materials

When setting stone directly on the ground, you'll get the best results using flat stones with a fairly consistent thickness. Another requirement is that the paving be heavy enough so that it can't be dislodged easily. Stones more than 1½ inches thick—including flagstones, fieldstones, and rubble with at least one flat side—and precast concrete stepping stones are good choices.

Most precast concrete stepping stones are 2 inches thick, in square or round shapes, with an exposed-aggregate surface. Others are poured into molds to simulate natural stones; these are referred to as "cultured" stone.

You can buy round stones up to 24 inches in diameter; square stones range from 12 to 48 inches. Space smaller stones 18 to 20 inches apart to accommodate an average stride. Larger stones (2 feet square or larger) can be butted together on firm, tamped soil or sand to form a solid walkway.

Laying Stone in the Ground

This section describes how to construct a stone walk without a gravel-and-sand base and without edgings. Select a good mix of large and small stones; fill spaces between large stones with small stones.

Outline the Walk. Lay out the edges of the walk, using stakes and string for straight walks or a rope or garden hose for curved walks, as described in "Forming a Curved Walk," page 87. Mark the ground with sand or flour, and remove the sod or loose topsoil within the walk area. Tamp the bottom of the excavation.

SETTING STONES IN THE GROUND

project

You can construct a stone walkway without first creating a gravel-and-sand base, but you will still have to do some excavating. The bed should be free of stones, twigs, and any other kind of debris. Ideally, the bed for this type of walkway should be just slightly higher than grade. If you are using thick, irregular stones, check your installation as you go along to make sure it is level.

TOOLS & MATERIALS

▌ Round-bottom shovel
▌ Work Gloves
▌ Flat-bottom shovel
▌ Rake ▌ Tamper ▌ Level
▌ Hammer and cold chisel
▌ Flat stones of a consistent thickness

1 Remove the grass and topsoil to an adequate depth so that the stone surfaces are slightly higher than the surrounding grade. Use a long level or straight board to ensure the stones are all about the same height when placed. Do a dry run, placing the stones in the pattern you want. Some trial-and-error fitting will be necessary to get a perfect layout.

2 Remove all of the stones, and trace the outline of the cornerstone in the soil below it. If possible, choose a larger, square-shaped stone for the corner to begin the walkway. Reset the cornerstone so that it sits approximately 1½ in. above grade. Where necessary, remove soil or place additional loose soil below the stone to obtain the proper depth.

3 Install the rest of the stones, using the cornerstone as a guide. Leave a gap of at least ½ in. between the stones. Check your work often using a level and straight-edge to make sure all of the stones are set at the same height. When all of the stones are set in place, fill the gaps with topsoil, and use a dowel or shovel handle to tamp it firmly in place.

WALKS ON A GRAVEL-AND-SAND BASE

Most walks last longer and fare the elements better when built on a base consisting of 2 inches of sand over 4 inches of gravel.

The best gravel for the job is compactible gravel because you can tamp it to form a well-drained, firm base. Crushed limestone with ¾ inch or smaller stones is ideal for this application. Avoid smooth river-run or pea gravel. When you buy the stone, figure on using 1 cubic yard for every 75 square feet of walk area.

Place a bed of builder's sand on top of the gravel base. The sand helps drain water away from the pavement and makes a smooth, level base that supports individual paving units. When ordering builder's sand, figure on using 1 cubic yard for every 150 square feet of walk area.

Although joints between paving units can be filled with topsoil or mortar, most often dry-laid walks have joints filled with mason's sand. This sand is finer than the builder's sand used for bedding the pavement. The amount of mason's sand needed depends on the size of the joints. For a standard brick walk, you will need a few cubic feet for every 100 square feet of walk area.

Plotting and Excavating the Subbase

Begin by determining the exact width of the walk. On a flat surface, such as a driveway, lay down several courses of the paving pattern you've chosen. Joints should be ⅛ inch or less for sand or ½ inch for topsoil. Measure across the pattern to determine the exact width of the walk. Then cut a piece of wood to that length and use it to check the spacing between the edging or temporary forms when you install them. The following explains how to lay out the path in step-by-step detail.

Locate the Edges of the Walk. At each end of the walk, drive two 1x2 stakes at least 2 feet into the ground to indicate the edges of the walk, and attach strings. Check to make sure that the strings are the same distance apart at both ends. If you want the walk to be square to some other element, such as a sidewalk or the wall of a house, make sure the lines are perpendicular to the element by using the 3-4-5 triangulation method. (See "Using the 3-4-5 Method," page 168.)

Establish the Walk's Height. Mark one stake at each end to indicate the walk's height. In most cases, this will be about 1 inch above ground level. A poured-concrete walk or dry-laid walk with irregularly shaped paving mate-

BUILDING FORMS

POSITION THE LAYOUT STRINGS to create a walk that is the width of the strings. If the walk requires forms, drive 2x3 stakes every 2 feet along the walk. For temporary forms, drive the stakes so that their inner edge is outside of the layout lines by the thickness of the form. Add the thickness of the form to the thickness of the edging to determine the location of the stakes.

If the edging will be a ribbon of concrete, drive two rows of stakes as shown in the inset. The outer face of the interior stakes should be inside the layout strings by the width of the form. Set the inner face of the second row of stakes outside the layout string by the width of the edging plus the thickness of the form.

Use galvanized nails or screws to fasten two-by forms to the stakes. Check the placement of the forms with a piece of wood cut to the width of the walk.

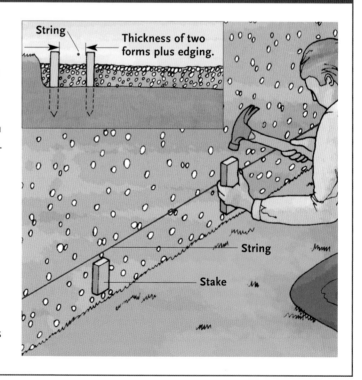

String

Thickness of two forms plus edging.

String

Stake

FORMING A CURVED WALK

1. Use a garden hose to lay out the curves. Mark the curves with spray paint or chalk.

2. Dig a trench along the edges with a shovel, deep enough so that the edging will rise above grade.

3. Set edging blocks into the trenches to contain the surface material and prevent erosion.

4. Spread gravel or other finishing material onto the walk in layers, and tamp each layer firmly.

rials, such as flagstones, should be pitched ¼ inch per foot along its width. Mark the walk height on one stake; then use a level to transfer this mark to the opposite stake. Adjust the second mark up or down to establish the pitch, and attach the strings to the stakes.

If drainage is a problem, slope the walk along its length as well. Use a line level to level the strings between the stakes. Measure down the stakes at the far end of the walk to get a ¼-inch-per-foot slope, and attach the strings at this point. (If the walk abuts a sidewalk, the low end of the walk should be level with it.) If the slope between the house and sidewalk is more than about 2 inches per foot, steps may be required. Check with the local building department for code requirements in your area.

Mark the Ground. Mark the location of the walk edges on the ground by sprinkling flour or sand over the strings. Mark the string locations on the stakes, and remove the strings so that they won't interfere when you dig the walk. Make sure the string marks are clear because you will reattach the strings later.

Excavate the Site. Use a pickax and shovel to remove the sod and dig a trench about 1 foot wider than the walk so that you have room to install edging. While digging, reattach the strings periodically to check the depth of the excavation; measure down from your layout strings. The trench needs to accommodate a 4-inch-deep gravel bed and whatever edging you will put on top of it. Use a hand tamper or power tamper to compact the soil.

Dry-Laid Walks

LAYING THE WALK

Once you dig out the sod, rake away any stones and twigs. The most difficult step will be creating the gravel and sand bed. The gravel must be firmly compacted: add one layer; compact it; add a second layer; and compact that, too. If you are adding edging, make sure it is deep enough to contain both the paving material and the sand layer.

TOOLS & MATERIALS

- Work Gloves ▮ Spade ▮ Rake or hoe
- Hand or mechanical tamper ▮ Broom
- Mallet and bedding board ▮ Garden hose
- Brick set for cutting bricks or pavers
- Landscape fabric ▮ Mason's sand
- Sand ▮ Screed board ▮ Edging material
- Edging spikes ▮ Pavers
- Material for forms if needed

1 After excavating the walk area, add 2 in. of gravel; rake it smooth; and tamp it. Add another 2 in., and tamp again. If you are installing edging, place enough gravel so that the edging is level with your layout string guides. If you are not using edging, add gravel until you have a 2-in. space below the string, plus the thickness of your paving material.

4 Make a screed board to level the sand. The screed board should be as wide as your walkway; its depth will be equal to the height of your pavers. If there are no forms to use as a guide for the screed, set up temporary guides on both sides of the walkway. Make a screed using two boards as shown. Otherwise, cut notches to fit in a 2x6 board.

5 Plastic edging strips were developed to create a strong, permanent, nearly invisible finished edge for pavers when no visible border is desired. Some strips are rigid for straight walks, while others are flexible enough to bend into curves for undulating walkways. Drive long spikes through the edging's perforations to hold it securely in place.

2 Roll out landscape fabric over the entire walk. The fabric should completely cover the subbase material under the pavers. Overlap the fabric by several inches where sections meet. Landscape fabric helps to retard weed growth, and it prevents the bedding sand from sinking into and disappearing through the spaces formed by the gravel below it.

3 Spread about 2 in. of sand over the fabric. Use a hoe or rake to smooth out the sand, but be careful not to disturb the fabric or pull it out of place. When smooth, use a fine water mist to dampen and settle the sand. Fill in any low spots, then re-mist. Build up the sand so that the paving material will be slightly higher than the finished walk height.

6 Before you complete the edging installation, test-fit rows of pavers at intervals to ensure that they will fit closely, but not too tightly, from one side of the walkway to the other. When you're ready to begin, start setting the pavers in one corner and work outward. As you proceed, bed each paver into the sand with a tap of a rubber mallet.

7 Continue installing the pavers. Be sure to maintain the proper joint distances between pavers. Some paving units have pre-formed lugs on all sides that automatically provide the right amount of spacing. If yours do not, leave a $\frac{1}{16}$ to $\frac{1}{8}$ in. gap to fill with sand. Joints between irregularly shaped pavers will vary, but try to maintain a consistent width. Continued on next page.

Dry-Laid Walks

Continued from previous page.

8 As you work, use a long level or straight board edge to ensure that your rows of pavers are about equal in height, but do not worry at this point if they are not perfectly even. To finish seating the pavers, rent a power tamper and make repeated passes over the entire surface. The pavers will level out as the tamper compresses them into the sand base.

9 To seat any pavers that remain raised, or "proud," lay a one-by board on the surface and pound the higher unit with a rubber mallet or hand sledge hammer until it is level with its neighbors. Don't worry about damaging the unit; the sand below will absorb most of the shock, and concrete pavers are extremely durable and difficult to break.

10 After all of the pavers are installed and leveled by the power tamper, spread a thin layer of fine, dry, mason's sand over the entire surface. Then use a stiff broom to sweep the sand into the joints. Sweep in all directions, making sure to completely fill the spaces between the pavers. Large, open joints also can be filled with topsoil or dry mortar.

11 Spray the walk with a fine water mist to settle the sand into the joints. Keep adding dry sand until it no longer disappears between the pavers. You may have to repeat this step several times before you are finished. After a week or two, or following a heavy rain, don't be surprised to see gaps appear. Reapply sand periodically to keep the joints filled.

Filling Wide Joints

Topsoil or mortar should be used in joints that are wider than ½ inch thick. To fill the joints with topsoil or mortar, lightly hose off the entire walk surface. When all standing water in the joints has disappeared, you can either pack the joints with topsoil and plant grass or a ground cover, or you can mortar the joints. For information on using this method see "Dry Mortar Method," page 108.

If you installed forms for an edging detail, carefully pull up any temporary forms and shovel gravel along the outside of the edging. Tamp the gravel, and fill the area with a few inches of topsoil. Be sure to cover any permanent stakes. If you used plastic edge restraints, cover them with topsoil, and seed or sod the filled-in area.

WALK EDGING OPTIONS

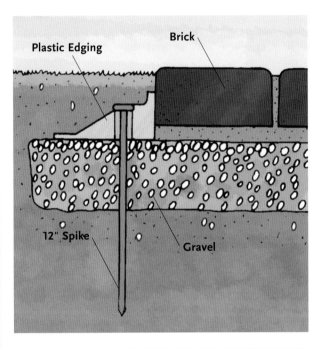

Plastic Edging · Brick · 12" Spike · Gravel

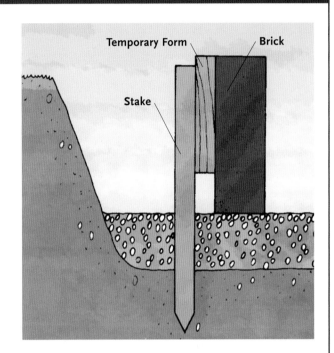

Temporary Form · Brick · Stake

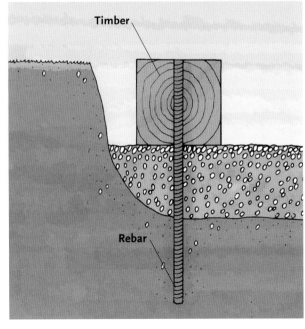

Timber · Rebar

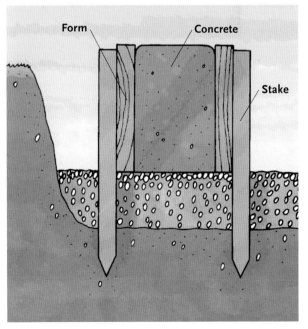

Form · Concrete · Stake

hard mortar-bed walks 6

SETTING PAVING UNITS IN MORTAR atop a hard concrete base is the most durable type of walk construction. Almost any pavers that can be set in sand can be set in mortar, including thin stone, brick, or concrete materials that could crack if bedded in sand. The mortar adheres the pavers to the concrete, and the solid base prevents them from sinking, buckling, or shifting. A rigid concrete base also minimizes ground movement, preventing mortared joints from cracking, but you can choose to fill the joints with sand or soil.

ANATOMY OF A MORTAR WALK

As with dry-laid walks, mortar-bed walks should be set on a firm, well-drained subbase. Depending on soil conditions, this subbase could be firmly tamped soil, but a preferable subbase consists of tamped gravel. The concrete base is placed on the gravel, mortar is spread over the concrete, and the paving materials are then bedded in the mortar.

Mortared walks are more difficult and expensive to build than dry-laid walks; however, there's less upkeep as long as the concrete base remains structurally sound. You can build a mortar-bed walk over either a new concrete base or an existing concrete walk.

SITE CONDITIONS

A new concrete base should be set low enough so that the finished walk surface is about 1 inch above the surrounding grade level. When measuring, bear in mind that the concrete is placed on a 4-inch-deep gravel base.

Make the concrete base as wide as the finished walk. Before you build the base forms, lay out a few courses of the paving material (with properly spaced joints) to determine the correct width. When you place the concrete, rough-float or broom the surface to provide a ragged but even base that will ensure good mortar adhesion. After the concrete has cured, simply apply mortar and pave over the slab. Edging isn't necessary, although you can add it for a finished look. If you include edging, adjust the depth and width of the excavation accordingly.

MATERIALS FOR A MORTAR-BED WALK

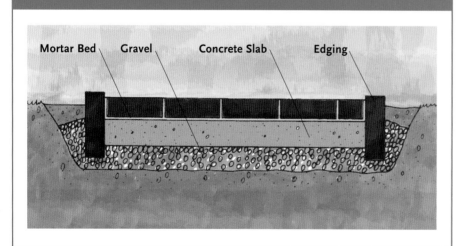

Mortar Bed   Gravel   Concrete Slab   Edging

A new mortared brick walk improves the approach to the entryway at the back of this older house, above. Its upkeep should be relatively easy.

Mortared joints surrounding slate slabs, opposite, should remain stable if the concrete base is installed properly.

USING AN EXISTING WALK

AN EXISTING CONCRETE-BASE WALK that is level and stable can be used as a base for new pavers. The new mortar bed will compensate for minor defects or irregularities in the old walk. Small holes should first be filled and leveled with concrete-patching material. Do not attempt to patch over a walk that is badly cracked or buckled, as this usually indicates unstable soil, a weak slab, or both.

If you pave over an existing walk, clean the surface thoroughly to remove any materials that could prevent the new mortar from adhering. Use a commercial driveway cleaner or a solution of 1 part trisodium phosphate (TSP) to 5 parts water. Scrub briskly with a push broom or stiff bristle brush; then rinse and allow to dry.

smart tip

DEALING WITH PAINTED CONCRETE

IF AN EXISTING WALK HAS BEEN PAINTED OR HAS A SLICK FINISH, BRUSH ON A SOLUTION OF MURIATIC ACID AND WATER USING A PUSH BROOM PRIOR TO ADDING A NEW MORTAR BED. YOU CAN ALSO APPLY A COAT OF CONCRETE BONDER USING A ROLLER. WEAR GLOVES AND GOGGLES WHEN USING MURIATIC ACID.

Brick set in a herringbone pattern forms an elegant walk that opens onto a pool-side patio. A border of neatly trimmed boxwood complements the brick with a different shape and texture.

MORTAR MIXES

FOR MOST MORTAR-BED WALK PROJECTS, it's more convenient to buy ready-mixed mortar, sold by the bag at building suppliers, than to mix your own. The mortar to use, called Type M, is noted for its high compressive strength and water resistance. Type M mortar consists of 1 part portland cement, ¼ part hydrated lime, and 3 parts sand. Local building codes may specify different proportions, depending on your climate. Also, local patio and masonry suppliers can advise you on the best mix for your particular area and application. Lime can stain certain kinds of stone. If your walk will be stone, buy a lime-free mortar mix or substitute fireclay for lime.

Follow the directions on the bag when mixing mortar. The amount of water required depends on the composition of the dry mixture, the width of the mortar joints or mortar bed, the absorption rate of the materials used, and the weather. Because of these many variables, you may have to do some experimentation to achieve the proper mix for your project. Use a wet mix if you are working with brick and concrete patio blocks, because they tend to absorb more water than stone and tile, which require a dry, or stiff, mix.

Tile and gauged stone are either set on a dry bed of mortar, which you wet later, or on latex-portland cement. You can make latex-portland cement mortar by combining the appropriate amount of liquid latex additive to portland cement and sand.

1 The quantity of mortar needed depends on the size of the walk and the type of pavers used. Large, irregular paving materials require a thicker mortar bed than thin, uniform-size pavers. For convenience, or for smaller projects, use ready-mixed Type M mortar, which is sold by the bag at building suppliers. If you buy separate quantities of cement, sand, and lime to make your own mortar, mix the dry ingredients together in a mortar box or tub and blend them thoroughly.

2 Generally, one 80-lb. bag of premixed mortar is sufficient for 15 square feet of walk. Adjust this quantity to suit the type of paving units you use. Add a small amount of water to the mix initially— mortar should be wet but not runny, with peaks that stand up when formed. Your project may require a slightly different mixture. For example, use a wetter mix for brick and concrete pavers. These materials absorb more water than stone and tile, which require a dry, or stiff, mix.

TOOLS FOR WORKING WITH MORTAR

To mix mortar you will need a hoe or shovel, wheelbarrow, and mortar mixing tub. You can also mix mortar on a flat, clean surface, such as a 4 x 4-foot piece of plywood. If your project will require a lot of mortar, renting a power mixer may be a practical idea. Because mortar sets up quickly (usually within 1 hour), mix only small amounts at a time—typically 3 cubic feet or less for mortar beds and ½ to 1 cubic foot for joints, depending on how fast you work.

To carry small amounts of mortar to the work area, you can use a mason's hawk or make a mortar board from a piece of plywood cut to a convenient size, such as 12 x 12 inches. You will also need several screed boards to level gravel, concrete, or the mortar bed. The gravel and concrete screeds are simply straight boards. For a mortar screed board, cut a 2x6 a few inches longer than the width of the walk you are building, and notch each end to equal the thickness of the paving material. (See "Using a Screed Board," page 73.)

Make sure to use the right mortar mix. A lime-free mortar is best for stone such as this.

Hard Mortar-Bed Walks

PREPARING PAVING MATERIALS

Whether they come from a stone yard or your backyard, stones tend to be covered with dirt, dust, and grit. Wash the stones with clear water, because any residue clinging to them will draw moisture from the mortar, weakening the bond. Before setting porous stones, such as sandstone, dampen them so that they don't suck moisture out of the mortar mix. Denser stones, such as Rocky Mountain quartzite, and sealed paver bricks may be set dry.

ABSORBENCY TEST

Because most face brick absorbs moisture quite readily, it should be wetted down before setting. Otherwise, the bricks will suck moisture out of the mortar base, resulting in a poor bond. You can check the absorbency of the bricks you're setting by putting 20 drops of water in one spot on a sample of the brick. Wait 90 seconds. If the water disappears, spray all of the bricks with a garden hose before you mix the mortar. Continue spraying until water runs out from the brick pile. By the time you get the mortar mixed, the surface water should have evaporated, leaving the bricks slightly damp to the touch.

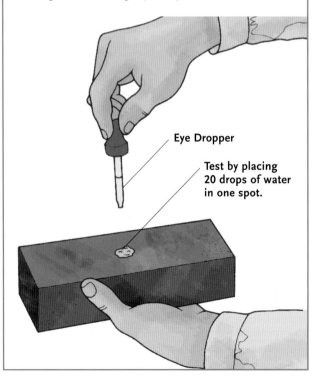

Eye Dropper

Test by placing 20 drops of water in one spot.

Using older brick or stone? Be sure to wash the material with water in order to remove dirt and grime.

smart tip

FORMS FOR CURVES

SET UP ANY STRAIGHT SECTIONS OF THE FORM WITH STANDARD LUMBER, BUT USE ⅛-INCH HARDBOARD FOR THE CURVED SECTIONS. TO REINFORCE THE BEND AGAINST THE CURING CONCRETE, INSTALL ADDITIONAL STAKES ALONG THE OUTSIDE EDGE OF THE FORM EVERY FEW INCHES.

PREPARING THE WALK

Drive stakes beyond your excavation, and use strings to mark the finished width of the concrete base. Build 2x4 forms to align with the strings, and set them on stakes 4 inches up from the bottom of the excavation. Attach the forms to the stakes with double-headed nails or screws that can be removed after the concrete sets and the forms are dismantled.

TOOLS & MATERIALS

▌Work gloves ▌Wheelbarrow
▌Shovels ▌Rakes ▌Tamper
▌Measuring tape ▌String and stakes
▌Lumber for forms ▌Level
▌Double-headed nails ▌Gravel
▌Screed ▌Wire mesh
▌Bolt cutters ▌Stones or bricks
▌Form release agent

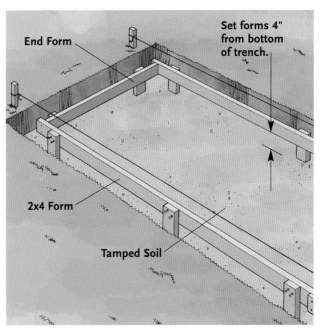

1 **Align the forms with the layout strings.** Drive stakes to the outside of the form boards, and be sure the stakes are below the tops of the forms. If the walk is longer than your boards, splice additional boards together with short pieces of 1x4. At each end of the walk, nail an end board between the side forms and stake each corner securely.

2 **After the forms are placed, spread the gravel evenly** in 1-in. layers, tamping each layer firmly to compact and level the gravel before adding the next layer. Allow the gravel to extend under and past the forms, and keep adding gravel until it is ½ in. below the bottom of the form boards. Rake or screed the gravel to make it smooth and level.

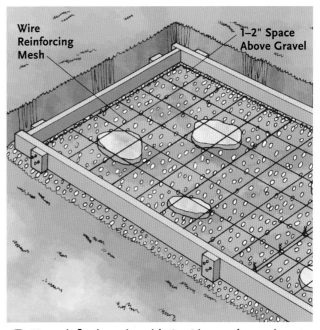

3 **Use reinforcing wire with 6 x 6-in. mesh openings to** strengthen the concrete slab. Cut the wire to fit inside the forms, overlapping long sections by 6 in. and using wire to tie overlapped pieces together. Place stones to raise the mesh about 2 in. above the gravel, or roughly in the center of the slab. Avoid walking on the mesh once it's in place.

POURING CONCRETE

Once you've set up the forms and added the base materials, thoroughly hose down the gravel the day before you pour the concrete. If any settling occurs, add more gravel, tamp it, and rescreed it.

If you're mixing and pouring the concrete by yourself, you can work at your leisure, mixing, pouring, and finishing one section of the walk at a time. To make working by yourself easier, put together a movable stop board. Divide the total length of the walk into equal sections; then mark the sections on the form boards. Position the stop board at the end of the first section; secure it with temporary stakes; and pour the concrete up to the board. After finishing the concrete surface, remove the stop board. You can pour the next section right up to the one you just finished or even leave the job for a few days and pick it up where you left it.

CONCRETE CHECKLIST

BECAUSE TIME IS LIMITED when you are pouring concrete, it's important to eliminate potential problems.

- **Provide access** for the concrete truck or wheelbarrows.
- **If you think that wheelbarrow traffic** might dislodge the form boards, build a ramp over them.
- **Check the forms** to be sure that they are level, spaced correctly, and fastened firmly to the stakes.

POURING THE CONCRETE BED

You may notice hollow spots on the surface of the walk after you've poured the concrete and screeded it. This is typical when pouring fresh concrete. To fill the hollow areas, simply add concrete to these spots and screed them, always pulling in the direction of the unfilled area. However, do not reuse concrete that has spilled outside the forms—and has come in contact with the soil. The concrete will have picked up dirt and other impurities and will weaken the finished project.

TOOLS & MATERIALS

- Expansion strips ▌Concrete
- Containers for mixing concrete
- Wheelbarrow ▌Shovels ▌Rakes
- Hoes ▌Screed

3 Use a hoe or rake to spread the concrete evenly in the form, chopping and blending the material as you work to eliminate air pockets. Tamp the concrete into corners and along the edges of the form, again to remove any voids. Use a shovel if necessary to even out high and low spots. The concrete fill should be even with the top edges of the form.

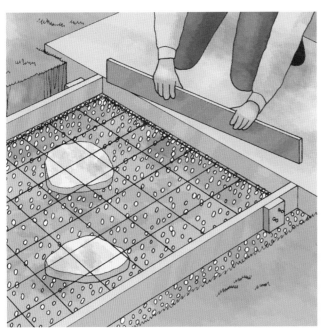

1 Finished concrete looks hard, but heat and cold cause it to expand and contract, so expansion strips (a compressible material available at masonry suppliers) are required. Place strips where the walk butts against existing structures, such as a house foundation, or at intervals in the walk as required by code. Do not cover strips with concrete. Caulk over the strips after the concrete cures.

2 Starting at the farthest point from your mixing area, pour concrete into the forms. If you use a wheelbarrow to transport the material, do not overfill it and risk spilling the concrete. Dump the concrete in mounds that extend about ½ in. above the tops of the forms. Avoid dumping loads on top of each other or in separate piles; instead, place each load against the previous load.

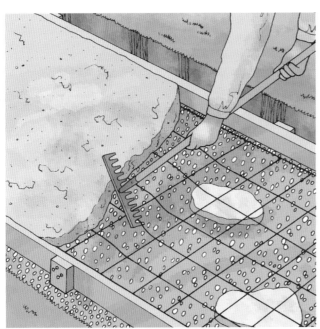

4 As you pour and spread the concrete, the weight of the material will press down the reinforcing mesh. Use your hoe or rake, or a pry bar or claw hammer, to pull up the mesh so that it remains in the center of the pour. Where necessary, add concrete and tamp to fill any voids under the mesh. Make sure the mesh does not protrude through the surface.

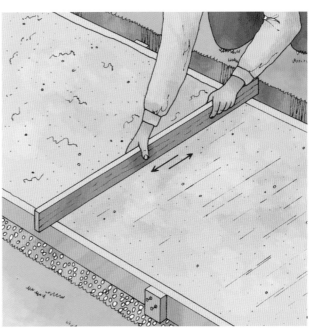

5 As you fill the form, use a screed board to strike off, or level, excess concrete above the tops of the form. Use a straight 2x4, approximately 1 ft. longer than the width of the form. Start at the beginning of the pour placing the screed firmly atop the form boards; then pull the screed forward along the forms in a side-to-side sawing motion.

project

FINISHING CONCRETE

Concrete that will be used as a base for a walk does not need to be perfectly smooth when finished. In fact, roughening up the surface a little will give the mortar used to attach the finish material some "tooth" to grab. However, you will need to level the surface and make sure the aggregate is embedded below the surface of the concrete. You'll use a large float for this step.

TOOLS & MATERIALS

▮ Darby ▮ Bull floats
▮ Trowels ▮ Wood float
▮ Stiff-bristle broom
▮ Paint roller (optional)
▮ Water from garden hose
▮ Plastic sheeting or canvas
▮ Concrete curing compound (optional)

1 After screeding, float the concrete with a darby to level it and embed any aggregate below the surface (use a long-handled bull float for large areas). Swing the darby in an arcing motion, and tilt the leading edge slightly upward to avoid digging into the wet concrete. Do not overwork the surface—when water starts to appear, you are done.

2 After floating the concrete, insert a pointed trowel between the forms and the slab, and slide the trowel along the forms to separate them from the concrete. Repeat this process after each smoothing operation. This will help when it's time to remove the forms.

3 Once the concrete is "thumbprint hard," use a wood trowel to roughen the surface. You can also drag a broom across the concrete to create an even rougher surface and provide more "tooth" for the mortar. Dampen and cover the concrete with plastic until cured (opposite).

CURING STRATEGIES

CONCRETE BEDS need either a rough-floated or broomed surface to ensure good mortar adhesion. You'll give the bed an initial floating and edging, then play a waiting game before finishing the surface. The amount of waiting time depends on climatic conditions—wind, humidity, temperature—and the type of mix used. As a general rule, you can start finishing the concrete as soon as the water sheen disappears from the surface and the concrete is hard enough to make a thumbprint about ¼ inch deep. If you start too soon, you'll notice excess water bleeding to the surface, which will weaken the slab. If you wait too long, the concrete won't smooth out at all, and you'll be stuck with the surface you have.

Curing Concrete

There are several ways to keep concrete moist, which is the key to the curing process. (See the three curing strategies that are shown at right.) The most common method is to apply a fine spray to the surface of the concrete. Coverage should be light, yet thorough. Keep the slab moist for about one week; be sure to check the slab several times a day. Reduce evaporation by covering the surface with plastic sheeting. Another option is to cover the concrete with water-saturated burlap or canvas. But be sure to keep the covering wet during the curing period by adding water periodically. This is especially important during hot, dry weather.

If the temperature drops below 50 degrees, continue curing for another 3 to 7 days. If you expect freezing weather, cover the slab with 6 to 12 inches of straw or hay covered with a tarp or plastic sheet. After about 10 days, remove the forms and backfill along the edges of the walk.

1 Apply a fine mist of water to the surface. Use caution—too much pressure can wash off the concrete finish.

2 Commercial curing compounds that you can apply with a roller or sprayer will help to retard moisture loss.

3 Cover the walk with plastic sheeting to keep moisture from escaping. Overlap sheet edges where they meet.

FINISHING THE WALK

project

After the concrete slab has cured, you can begin setting the mortar bed on it. Laying a brick path is shown here, but the process is similar for any masonry material. If you are working with irregularly shaped stones, plan on spending additional time deciding which stone goes where.

TOOLS & MATERIALS

- Work gloves ▌Wheelbarrow
- Paving bricks or other paving materials
- Edging or lumber for form and stakes
- Hammer and nails for form
- Mallet ▌Measuring tape and saw
- Mason's and notched trowels
- String and line level
- Mortar mix ▌Grout bag
- Striking tool

1 For a brick walk, install bricks on edge to form a border that will help hold the walk materials in place. If you are using other paving materials, you can install brick edging or temporary 2x4 forms. Install the forms on both sides (not on top) of the concrete slab. Set one side to equal the thickness of the mortar bed and pavement, and set the other side slightly higher to pitch the walk (at ⅛ in. per foot of width) for water runoff.

4 Start at one corner. Set the pavers into the mortar using a slight twisting motion. Avoid pressing so hard that the mortar squeezes out from under them. Set bricks with a firm tap of a trowel handle; larger stones may require a firmer tap from a rubber mallet. Use a guide string to keep squared pavers aligned and a level to check that all of them are bedded at the same height.

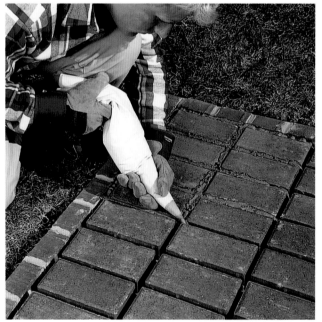

5 To fill the joints after the pavers are in place, mix a batch of mortar that is thin enough to pour but not too soupy or watery. (If you are mixing your own, combine 1 part cement to 3 parts sand.) Use a grout bag to squeeze the mortar into the joints or a coffee can to pour it in. Avoid getting mortar on the face of the paving materials, and clean up as you go.

2 Do a dry run with the paving material before applying mortar. This will help you adjust the spacing of the pavers to establish a pattern and avoid unnecessary cutting. Use ⅜- or ½-in.-thick wood strips to space bricks. Joints between irregular stones can be from ½ to 1½ in. wide. Joints for dimensioned stones should be no more than 1 in. wide.

3 Wet the slab before applying mortar. Mix enough mortar to cover a section about 3 x 4 ft. Use a notched trowel to spread the mortar evenly over the entire area. The mortar bed should be a minimum of ½ in. thick for bricks and dimensioned stone, and at least 1 in. thick for paving materials of varying thickness, such as flagstone.

6 Before the mortar hardens, use a trowel to strike off, or remove, any excess grout; then use a wood dowel or jointing tool to finish the joints. Draw the tool over each joint to compress the mortar in place and produce a slightly concave indentation. Avoid making deep, recessed joints that will trap dirt and water and create an irregular walk surface.

7 Again, use a trowel to remove mortar that has squeezed out of the joints. Wait several hours to allow the joints to set; then brush off any loose mortar with a whisk broom. Remove any mortar smears with a damp sponge or wet burlap. After a week, clean any mortar haze from the walk with a stiff brush and a TSP solution (½ cup to one gal. of water). Rinse thoroughly.

DRY MORTAR METHOD

RATHER THAN MIXING A BATCH OF MORTAR and pouring it into the joints, many stonemasons use a dry-mortar method to save time and labor. If you live in a warm climate, where freeze-thaw conditions are not a concern, you can use this method to fill joints between bricks, blocks, or stones.

1 Mix and spread the mortar after cleaning the walk surface. Mix 1 part portland cement with 3 parts sand, or use bags of premixed mortar. Spread the dry mortar evenly over the walk area; then sweep it into the joints using a stiff broom.

2 Force mortar into the joints by using a short piece of wood to pack the dry mixture firmly between the pavers. Sweep in more dry mix, if necessary, and continue packing the joints until the mortar in the joints is flush with the surrounding paving material.

3 Moisten the joints by setting the nozzle on a garden hose to spray a fine mist, dampening the mortar. Gently soak the joints. Be careful not to flush the mortar out, and don't allow pools of water to form. Over the next hour, periodically mist with a hose.

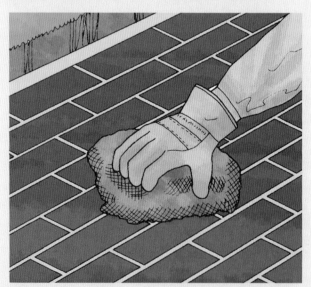

4 To finish the joints, wait until the mortar hardens slightly. At this point, you can either tool concave joints with a convex jointer or strike the joints flush with a trowel. When the mortar dries, clean the excess off the stones with a damp piece of burlap.

smart tip

PROTECT YOUR LAWN

RUNNING A HEAVY WHEELBARROW FULL OF CONCRETE, STONES, OR BRICKS BACK AND FORTH ACROSS YOUR YARD CAN RUIN THE LAWN. OFTEN THE ONLY RECOURSE IS TO RESEED OR RESOD THE ENTIRE AREA AFTER INSTALLING THE WALK. TO PROTECT THE GRASS AND GROUNDS AROUND THE WORK SITE, MIX CONCRETE AND CUT AND STORE MATERIALS ON TARPS ON THE DRIVEWAY. TO TRANSPORT MATERIALS, LAY A SERIES OF PLANKS AND PLYWOOD SHEETS ALONG THE IN-TENDED SUPPLY ROUTE. THIS WILL SAVE WEAR AND TEAR ON THE LAWN, AND YOU WILL FIND IT EASIER TO PUSH A HEAVY WHEELBARROW OVER THE WOOD THAN THROUGH SOFT SOIL.

You can keep cuts to a minimum if you lay out the bricks in a dry run—even if it's a complex pattern.

smart tip

CUTTING BRICKS BY HAND

IT IS EASIER TO USE A CIRCULAR SAW WITH A MA-SONRY BLADE TO MAKE COMPLICATED CUTS. BUT FOR ONLY A FEW SIMPLE CUTS, MAKE THEM BY HAND. MARK A CUT LINE ON THE BRICK, ALLOWING FOR THE JOINT SPACE, AND SCORE THE LINE WITH A CHISEL. TO MAKE THE CUT, TAP A BRICK SET PLACED OVER THE LINE LIGHTLY BEFORE DELIVERING A HEAVY BLOW.

Hard Mortar-Bed Walks

A long, reddish brown brick walkway that leads the eye straight to the front door exists in contrast to the gray stone that was used on the face of this house. When chosen thoughtfully, mixed materials can create a handsome result.

CERAMIC AND STONE TILE

Tile—either stone or ceramic—lends a formal look to a walk and often is used to make an indoor-outdoor connection. Tile is expensive, however, and many kinds aren't suited for outdoor use. Generally, climatic conditions in your area will dictate which outdoor tiles will be carried at local tile dealers and stone yards.

Unless you're tiling an existing concrete walk, choose the tile first, then lay out the walk based on the tile size. Most tile dealers will loan you a few samples for this pur-pose. Sizes for square tiles range from 4 inches to 24 inches; other shapes include rectangles, hexagons, oc-tagons, and curved ogee profiles. Ceramic floor tiles usu-ally look best with mortared joints spaced ⅜ to ¼ inch apart. Stone tiles can be either butted together with swept-sand joints or spaced for mortared joints.

Although most ceramic and stone tiles are extremely dense, they are also brittle and thin (⅜ to ¼ inch thick), so they require a perfectly smooth, flat, and sturdy concrete base. Rather than being set in mortar, tiles are set in spe-cial thin-set cement tile adhesive. Consult the tile dealer or manufacturer for the appropriate type of adhesive.

SUITABLE TYPES OF TILE

IN MOST OUTDOOR SITUATIONS you'll want a tile that doesn't absorb too much water—one that can go through the freeze-thaw cycle without cracking. You'll also want tiles that won't become slippery when wet. Some tile manufacturers use a labeling system devised by the International Standards Organization that makes it clear which tiles are best. A snowflake on the box indicates that the tile is freeze-thaw resist-ant. A footprint means the tile stands up well to foot traffic, and a hand means the tile is for walls only. Without the labels, however, it's very hard to tell from the box whether a given tile is good for outdoor use. Fortunately, some categories of tile have proven them-selves for outdoor use. Unglazed quarry tile, unglazed pavers, and gauged stone are all tiles that work well outdoors.

Unglazed Quarry Tile. This category includes any hard, red-bodied ceramic floor tile of consistent di-mensions, no less than ⅜ inch thick. Most are vitreous (glossy in appearance) or semivitreous. The tile body (called the bisque) is usually a deep brick red, al-though pigments may be added to produce other col-ors, usually earth tones or pastels.

Unglazed Pavers. All tiles that are not classified as quarry tiles are called unglazed pavers, although the terms are sometimes used interchangeably. Pavers range from impervious porcelain varieties to nonvitre-ous clay. Use the densest you can find. These pavers are usually uniform in size and dimension and come in a wide variety of colors and surface textures.

Cement-Bodied Tile. As the name implies, these tiles are made of cement. Extruded cement-bodied tiles are extremely dense and offer strong resistance to wear. Tiles made for outdoor use are treated with a sealer that must be reapplied periodically.

Gauged Stone. Slate, marble, and granite come as gauged stone tiles. They are cut to precise shapes (squares or rectangles) and sizes, and they're ground to uniform thickness. The surface may be left natural or machine-polished to a high sheen. Set much like ce-ramic tile, gauged stone is extremely expensive and is used for interior floors, walls, and countertops. How-ever, you can use it to make an indoor-outdoor con-nection, such as extending a stone floor in a foyer out to a front porch. For outdoor use, avoid stones with smooth, slick surfaces.

Cutting Tiles. If you have a lot of tiles to cut, it's best to rent a wet saw. This tool is also handy if you have many irregular cuts to make. Check your local hardware store or home center. Renting a wet saw is not expensive and it is well worth doing so.

If you need to cut only a few tiles, use a hacksaw with a carbide-grit blade to make a groove in the face of the tile about ¹⁄₁₆ inch deep along the cut line. (Very thick tiles may require a second cut on the backside.) Place the tile over a wood dowel or length of heavy in-sulated wire, and press down sharply on either side to snap the tile. (See "How To Cut Tiles," page 112.)

A tile walk with decorative insets requires careful planning and precise cutting.

SETTING A TILE WALK

project

Use either a dry-set mortar or latex-portland cement mix to set tile and gauged stone. Check with your tile supplier or manufacturer for the appropriate application requirements. Ideally, mortar should be applied on a warm day but out of direct sunlight to prevent it from setting up too quickly.

TOOLS & MATERIALS

- Garden hose
- Mortar
- Mixing tub
- Mortar hoe
- Flat trowel
- Notched trowels
- Tile
- Tile saw
- Lumber for jig
- Tile spacers
- Level
- Rubber mallet
- Grout
- Grout bag or rubber float
- Striking tool
- Damp cloth

HOW TO CUT TILES

ONE WAY TO MAKE A CUT BY HAND is to use a hacksaw with a carbide-grit standard flat blade. As shown in the illustration below, this type of cut is easy to make. Basically, you score the tile and then apply pressure to make a clean break at the cut line.

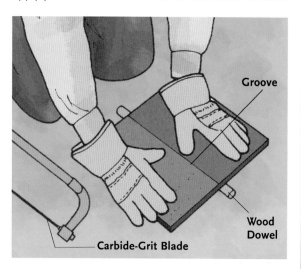

Groove

Wood Dowel

Carbide-Grit Blade

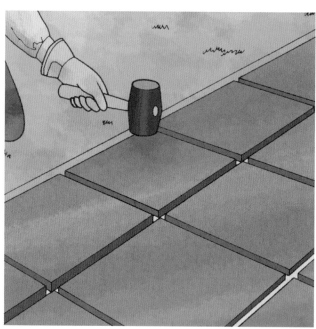

3 As you lay the tiles, and before the mortar hardens, use a rubber mallet or a hammer with a wood block to bed the tiles into the mortar. Tap lightly on the center of each tile; then recheck the tiles for alignment and level. Allow the mortar to harden for a day or two before grouting the joints.

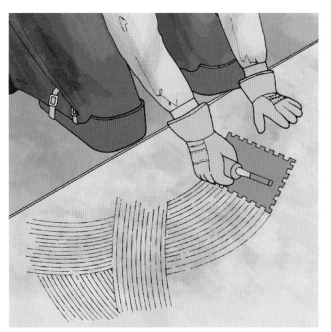

1 Using a flat trowel, first apply a ¼-in. "scratch coat" of mortar over the concrete slab and allow it to dry. This creates a smooth, level base for the thin tiles and stone, which are more easily cracked than thicker paving units. Next, use a ½-in. notched trowel to apply a second coat, on which you'll bed the pavers while the mortar is still wet.

2 Starting at one end of the walk, lay the tiles in the desired pattern. To maintain uniform joint spaces, make a jig as shown by nailing short lengths of wood (equal to the joint widths) to a 1x4 that is slightly longer than the walk's width. Place a level atop this gauge, and check both the spacing and tile height as you work to ensure a flat, consistent layout.

4 To fill the joints, use a premixed grout or mix 3 parts sand to 1 part portland cement. Add water until the mix is easy to pour but not soupy. Use a can with its rim bent into a spout, or a grout bag, to pour the mixture into the joints. You can also use a rubber float to force the mortar into the joints.

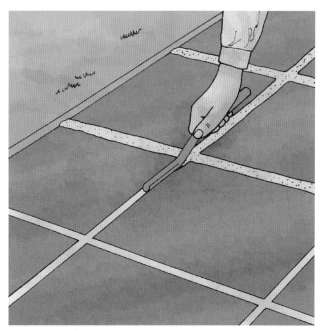

5 Before the mortar hardens but soon after it sets up (about 20 minutes), use a flat trowel to strike off any excess from the face of the tiles; then wipe the surface with a coarse, damp cloth. Smooth the joints using a dowel or striking tool to create a slightly concave profile. Clean the surface again to remove any mortar smears.

building stairways 7

IF THE GROUND LEVEL OF YOUR WALK changes dramatically or if your patio is terraced into the side of a hill, a set of steps needs to be part of your design. While it requires a little thought, some math, and a careful layout, you'll find that the actual construction is simple.

Exterior stairways are generally less steep than interior ones, but they are wider, and the rise between steps is smaller, making navigation easier in bad weather. The exact design of the stairway you build will depend on the terrain, but all stair designs have certain elements and construction basics in common with one another.

Building Stairways

DESIGN BASICS

Stairways must be wide enough to accommodate the traffic they have to handle. Four-foot-wide stairs are usually adequate for one person to stroll comfortably. Two people walking abreast need stairs that are 5 to 6 feet wide. Stairs in the middle of walks should be the same width as the walks.

Stairs leading to entries, decks, and patios should be wide enough to complement the scale of their surroundings. Build narrow stairs for a small patio—they'll look proportionate and will easily handle the traffic. A large patio may call for stairs that are wider than strictly necessary. The extra width accommodates the occasional crowd and helps keep the stairs in scale with the surroundings.

Finding the Run and Rise

Before you can figure tread/riser relationships, you need to compute the total rise and the total run. The total rise is the height between the lowest and highest levels of the stairs. The run is the horizontal distance from one end of the stairs to the other.

If the stairs run from a walk to a patio or deck, you get the rise by measuring the height of the structure. If the stairs go up a hillside, drive a tall stake into the ground at what will be the bottom of the stairs and a short stake at the top. Each stake should be plumb, and the tops should be at about the same height. Tie a string to the upper stake at ground level, then tie the string to the lower stake. Level the string with a line level, and measure the distance at the tall stake from the ground to the string—this equals the rise. To find the run, measure the horizontal distance between the stakes.

TREAD/RISER RELATIONSHIPS

ALL STAIRS HAVE TWO CRITICAL DIMENSIONS. The tread depth is measured from the front to the back of the tread—the part of the stairs on which you walk. Technically, tread depth is called the "unit run." The height of the individual stairs is equally important and is called the "unit rise." Typically, the higher the unit rise, the shallower the tread. As a rule of thumb for exterior stairs, the combined length of one tread and two rises should be 25 to 27 inches.

The maximum rise between any two steps should be between 5 and 7 inches—that's a comfortable step up for most people. This leaves a tread depth of between 11 and 17 inches. Many landscape designers believe that the best tread/riser proportion for garden stairs is a 15-inch tread with a 6-inch riser.

Landings. Where a set of steps is at a right angle to a walk or driveway, there should be at least a 3-foot landing between the stairway and the walk or drive. If a door or gate opens toward a landing or porch, the landing should be the width of the door plus at least 3 feet. Landings should be the same width as the treads.

Common Tread/Riser Relationships

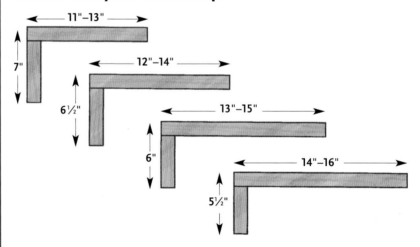

Rise and Run

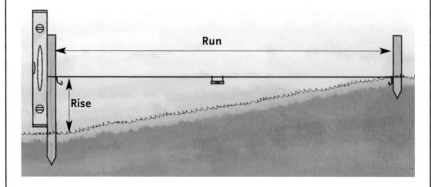

DETERMINING TREAD AND RISER SIZES

ONCE YOU KNOW THE RISE AND RUN, you can figure out the tread and unit rise. To determine the unit rise, divide the total rise by the potential number of stairs. Remember, the ideal unit rise is between 5 and 7 inches. If your answer is outside this range, adjust the number of steps. For example, if the total rise is 39 inches and you have five steps in mind, you'll need a riser height of 7¹³⁄₁₆ inches (39÷5=7.8)—too big for outdoor use. Six steps would give you a riser height of 6½ inches (39÷6=6.5), well within the right range.

Once you know the unit rise, calculate tread depth.

Remember, the tread depth plus twice the unit rise should be between 25 and 27 inches. (Twice the riser height in our example is 13 inches; subtracting that from 25 and then from 27 tells you that the treads should be between 12 and 14 inches deep.) Choose the depth that will give you the proper run.

If the rise and run won't work out to something that fits the formula, you usually have flexibility about where the top and the bottom of the stairway can be located. If it's necessary, you can adjust the total run to create a stairway that has a comfortable rise-and-run ratio.

Increasing the depth of the bottom-stair tread created a comfortable landing and transition onto a gravel driveway.

WOODEN STAIRWAYS

On steep or irregular slopes or where there are severe grade changes, raised wooden steps can often provide a bridge with little or no excavation or grading required. On gentle slopes, you can outline each step by laying landscape timbers directly on the ground and filling the spaces between them with smooth stones, bricks, poured concrete, or other suitable walk materials.

Stairway on Grade. The set of steps shown below are supported by a notched wooden stringer to which the treads are nailed. The stringer lays directly on the same type of sand-and-gravel base that supports the rest of the walk. Concrete footings at each end of the stairway anchor it in place.

Building Steps. Drive a stake at each of the corners of the stairway, and connect them with string to locate the stairway on the ground. To build a support for the bottom end of the stringers, you'll have to excavate a 10-inch-deep trench. It should extend about 6 inches beyond the sides of the steps. Fill the trench with a 6-inch layer of gravel, and tamp it. Then install a 2x4 form; fill the trench with concrete; and level the concrete by pulling a screed across the forms.

BUILDING A WOODEN STAIRWAY

project

Stringers are usually made from 2x12 stock. Lay out a single stringer using a framing square before making any cuts. After you cut the first stringer, use it as a template for cutting the second.

TOOLS & MATERIALS

- Shovels ■ Gravel
- Gravel tamper ■ Concrete mixing tools
- Concrete ■ Anchor bolts
- Masking tape ■ Framing square
- Pencil ■ Lumber for stringers
- Circular saw ■ Handsaw
- Hammer ■ Steel framing angles
- Lumber for risers and treads

STAIRWAY ON GRADE

In this cutaway, you can see the positions of the concrete footings at the top and bottom corners of one side of the steps. Steel framing anchors, which can be J- or L-shaped, are bolted to the footings and attached to stringers at each corner to hold the stairway in place. Notice the gravel base, which is the same type that provides additional support for the walk.

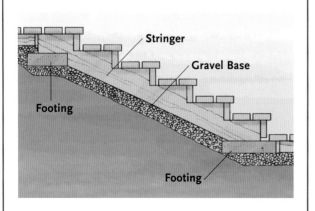

Stringer

Gravel Base

Footing

Footing

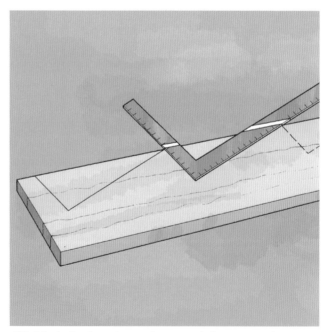

3 Mark the first rise and run, and then move the square down the stringer to mark the other dimensions. Each set of marks indicates a notch that will be cut for "open" stringers, where the treads rest atop the stringer and overlap its width. The same layout is used for uncut or "closed" stringers, where the treads butt against the inside faces of the stringers.

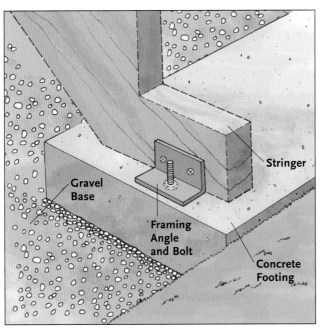

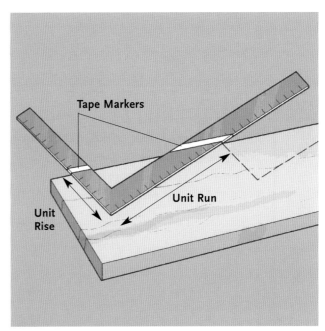

1 When you pour a concrete footing for outdoor stairs, measure carefully and place anchor bolts in the concrete while it is still wet. These bolts typically have a J- or L-shaped bottom to prevent them from twisting or pulling loose later. Anchor bolts have threaded tops with hex nuts to connect to metal framing angles that attach to the stringers.

2 To lay out a stringer, place tape on a carpenter's framing square to mark the rise and run for each step, also called the unit rise and unit run. This will allow you to position the square and mark the exact same dimensions for each step along the entire stringer. Measure and mark the unit run on the longest arm of the square; mark the unit rise on the square's shorter arm.

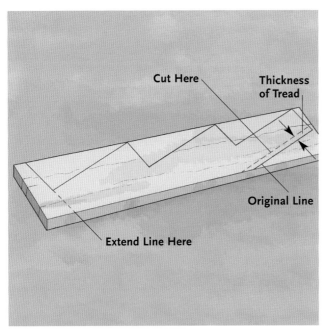

4 The framing square layout indicates the position of the treads as they sit atop the long, or "run," line. Allow for the thickness of each tread, which adds to the height of each rise. To do this, remove a section from the bottom of the stringers that is equal to the treads' thickness. Mark and cut the stringers as shown in the illustration above.

5 Use a circular saw and a handsaw to cut the first stringer. Then use this stringer as a template to mark and cut the other stringers. For stairways with tread widths that are more than 30 in. across, one or more intermediate stringers are usually necessary for stability and safety. Consult your local building codes for the required dimensions.

BUILDING A LANDSCAPE STAIRWAY

project

If your steps will be along a grade, you can often build them directly on the ground without a stringer. The stairway shown here will work well on a hillside where the run equals 24 to about 32 inches per foot of rise.

TOOLS & MATERIALS

▌ Lumber for stakes ▌ Measuring tape
▌ Line level ▌ Mason's twine
▌ Shovels ▌ Picks ▌ Landscape timbers
▌ Power drill-driver with ½-inch bit
▌ Rebar and landscape spikes
▌ Handheld sledge ▌ Gravel
▌ Landscape fabric (optional)
▌ Sand ▌ Bricks ▌ Screed
▌ Mason's sand ▌ Stiff-bristle broom
▌ Garden hose

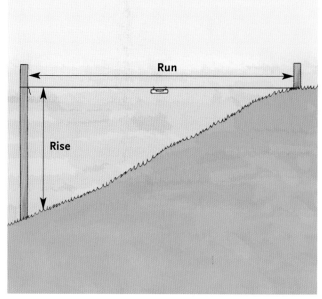

1 To build outdoor steps without footings or stringers, first measure the rise and run for the entire stairway from the bottom to the top of the slope. Drive a stake at the top, and stretch a line to a pole placed at the bottom end of the slope. Make sure the pole is vertically plumb and the line is level, and then measure the total rise and the run as shown.

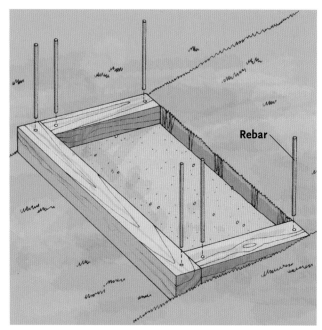

4 Next, you'll have to secure the first set of landscape timbers in place. To do this, drill ½-in. pilot holes, and then drive 18-in.-long sections of rebar through the timbers and directly into the soil. If there will be successive wood-on-wood stair courses, you'll have to drill pilot holes and then drive in 12-in.-long landscape spikes through the timbers.

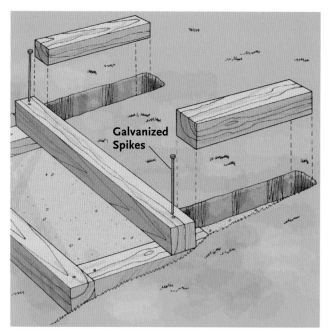

5 Dig trenches for the next riser and timbers as you go. Use a hand sledgehammer to drive in the spikes that secure these timbers to the course below. Pre-drilling holes for spikes is not always necessary, but doing so makes it easier to drive them home without heavy pounding, which can strain your muscles and possibly jostle the timbers out of place.

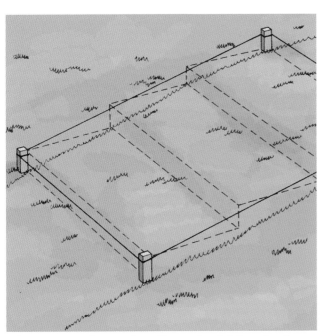

2 Compute the number of steps by dividing the rise by 6 in. (the nominal height of a 6x6 landscape tie). This example has a tread depth of 24 to 32 in., which allows for a comfortable, safe walking gait, an important consideration for outdoors. Mark the location of the stairway by driving stakes at the corners and stretching string between them.

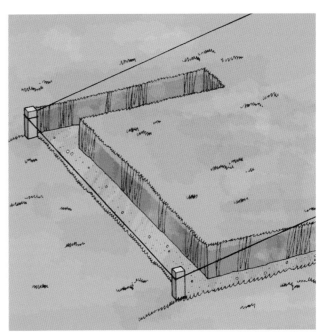

3 Dig the trenches for the first riser and side timbers. The side pieces support the next risers in turn. When buying landscape ties for outdoor steps, specify wood specially treated for ground contact. You can position the timbers directly on the earth, or dig a few inches and place a bed of gravel in the trench to help level the timbers and allow water to drain away.

6 Infill the treads with a 2-in.-deep layer of gravel topped by a 2-in. bed of sand. Before placing these materials, an optional layer of landscape fabric may be laid to block weed growth. Lay bricks in place, but do not press them into the sand. After all the bricks are installed, bed them by placing a 1x6 board across the surface and tapping with a mallet.

7 When you have completed all of the steps, use a stiff broom to sweep dry mason's sand into the brick joints. Sweep in all directions to fill any gaps, replenishing with additional sand as you go. Wet the surfaces with a light spray from a garden hose. Gaps will appear as the sand washes into the joints. Add sand and repeat the process as needed.

BUILDING A CONCRETE STAIRWAY

project

Concrete steps work well with sloped landscapes. You'll have to dig a flat-bottom trench into the hillside and line it with gravel. Then build a stair-shaped form that molds the concrete into one long stairway. Concrete garden stairs require a footing. (For more information on footings, see Chapter 9, "Footings for Walls," beginning on page 140.)

TOOLS & MATERIALS

- Line level ▍ Shovels and picks
- Stakes and layout string ▍ Framing square
- Measuring tape ▍ Lumber for forms
- Circular saw ▍ Clean masonry rubble
- Hammer and double-headed nails
- Lumber for braces ▍ Wire mesh
- Rebar ▍ Concrete ▍ Hoe or rake ▍ Screed
- Darby ▍ Edger ▍ Wooden float

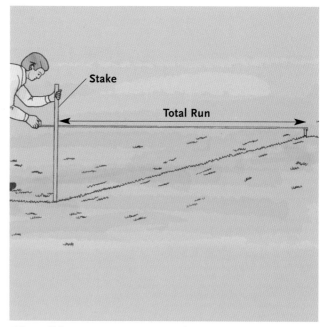

1 Building concrete steps outdoors requires more time and effort than it takes to construct other types of landscape stairways. The process is more exacting, but the number of steps required to do the job is the same as those necessary to build the stairs on the previous pages of this chapter. To determine the run, stretch a level string between stakes at the top and bottom of the hill.

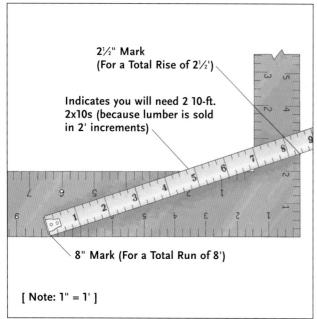

2½" Mark
(For a Total Rise of 2½')

Indicates you will need 2 10-ft. 2x10s (because lumber is sold in 2' increments)

8" Mark (For a Total Run of 8')

[Note: 1" = 1']

4 Although concrete forms are only temporary, they must be sturdy enough to contain the weight and pressure of poured concrete. Use 2x12 board lumber to make the forms, and be sure to place a sufficient number of stakes to hold them securely in place. To estimate the length of your form's sides, use a framing square and a measuring tape (using the scale 1 in. equals 1 ft.).

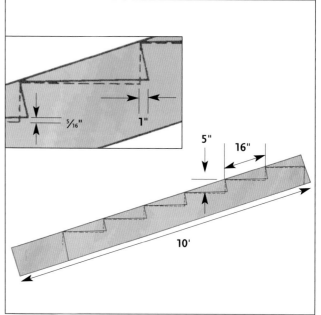

5 To allow rainwater and snowmelt to quickly drain, treads should slope slightly downhill. Allow a slope of about ¼ in. per foot of tread depth. Interior stairs usually have overhanging treads to prevent stubbed toes and heels from catching. This can't be done with concrete steps, so simply slant the bottom of the risers inward 1 in. for safety.

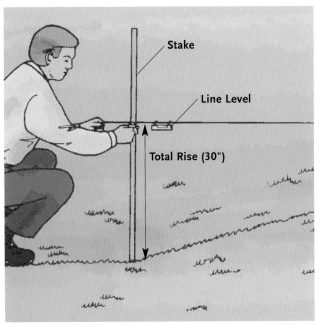

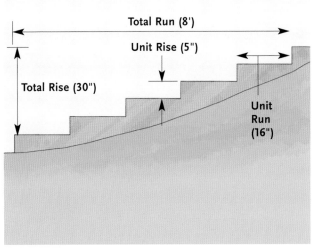

2 Next, find the rise by measuring up from the ground to the string on the downhill stake. Concrete garden stairs require a footing at the bottom and an additional one at the top for flights of three or more steps. This footing is typically wider than the walk itself. In areas where freezing occurs, footings must be placed at least 6 in. below the frost line.

3 After you determine the rise and run, divide the rise and then the run by the intended number of stairs to find a safe riser/tread relationship. The ideal riser height for outdoor stairs is 6 in. As a general rule, the combined length of one tread and two risers should equal 25 to 27 in., so treads with 6-in. risers should be from 13 to 15 in. deep.

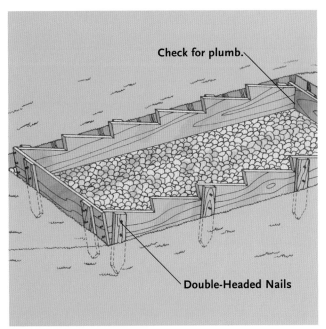

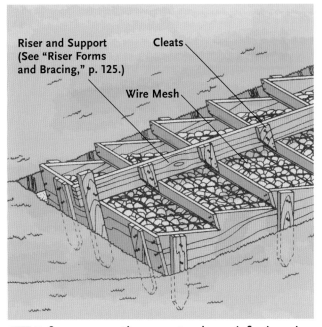

6 Excavate the trench for your footing to the required depth. Local codes may require installing a gravel layer beneath the concrete, so be sure to allow for this when you dig. However, a gravel base is recommended in any case because it will dissipate any groundwater that collects below the footing. Use stakes fastened with double-headed nails to secure the forms.

7 Before you pour the concrete, place reinforcing wire mesh in the excavation to add strength and integrity to the concrete, and to prevent the concrete from cracking. When the concrete is poured, use a hoe or rake to lift the mesh so that it is not compressed flat by the weight of the concrete and to ensure that it ends up in the middle of the pour. Continued on next page.

Building Stairways

Continued from previous page.

8 Begin pouring the concrete at the bottom of the stairway. Pour in sections, or lifts, that can be managed easily. Use a shovel to tamp and spread the material to eliminate air pockets and voids. Make sure to work the concrete into all corners of the forms and even out the coverage. Press any reinforcing mesh back into the mix if it rises to the surface.

9 Place enough concrete in each section of the forms so that it is equal to or slightly higher than the form sides. Start at the top stairs using a straight 2x4 at least 2 ft. wider than the stairs to screed the concrete level with the tops of the forms. Wide stairs will require a helper. As you work, shovel in additional wet concrete to fill any low spots.

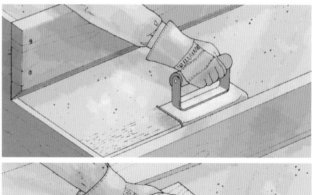

10 After screeding to level off each stair, and before the concrete has begun to harden, use a long wooden darby to smooth the surface. Make sweeping arcs across the concrete with the tool, but try to keep the edge flat to prevent pulling the wet mix out of the forms. Add small amounts of concrete to replenish low spots or voids if they appear.

11 When the concrete begins to set up, round off all exposed sides using a concrete edger (top). Give the surface a final smoothing with a wooden float. If a rougher texture is desired, pull a stiff-bristle broom across the surface. One day after the concrete is poured, remove the forms, but keep the concrete moist for a week to allow the concrete to cure.

RISER FORMS AND BRACING

TO MAKE A RISER FORM, rip two-by stock to equal the rise of the steps. For "Building a Concrete Stairway," page 122, rip 2x6s to 5 inches wide. When you make the rip cuts, set the blade of your saw to 45 degrees to create a bevel. Place the bevel to the outside at the bottom, so you can reach the entire tread when you pour and finish the concrete. Cut the riser forms to the width of the steps, plus 3 inches to accommodate the width of the side forms.

Nail the riser forms across the side forms. To brace the form, lay a 2x6 up the stairs, centered side to side. Cut cleats with ends angled at 45 degrees. Place a cleat against each riser form, and nail it to the brace. Toenail the cleat to the risers. Toenail the brace to the uphill end of the form with no cleat. Coat the forms with a release agent to keep concrete from sticking to them.

smart tip

SLIP-RESISTANT STEPS

MAKE YOUR STEPS SAFER BY CREATING A SLIP-RESISTANT FINISH. YOU CAN EMBED AGGREGATE IN THE CONCRETE, OR BRUSH THE UNCURED SURFACE WITH A BROOM. BELOW IS A STAMPED CONCRETE PRODUCT.

Depending on how you finish it, concrete can be an attactive choice for steps. A bullnose edge on the treads here refines the look.

The simplicity of this stairway suits this home's Asian-inspired landscaping. Concrete offered an ideal material for working with the site.

Building Stairways

BUILDING A BRICK STAIRWAY ON CONCRETE

project

Mortared brick steps sit on a concrete base that keeps the bricks and joints from cracking as the ground moves with the weather. To build brick stairs, follow the directions for building concrete stairs, but add to your excavation depth the height of the bricks plus ½ inch for the mortar bed that will hold the bricks on the concrete.

TOOLS & MATERIALS

- Work gloves
- Bricks or pavers
- Notched trowel
- Pointed trowel
- Type M or Type S ready-mix mortar
- Rounded jointer
- Garden hose
- Stiff-bristle brush

1 Lay out a test run on the concrete base to check the spacing of the brick pavers. (See "Brick Steps," opposite.) Adjust the joint widths if necessary, but keep brick joints to a consistent size. Mortar joints up to about 1 in. wide look best with standard-size bricks; joints wider than 1 in. may be weaker. Bricks laid flat handily accommodate tread widths built to multiples of 8 in.

2 Trowel and smooth a 1-in.-deep layer of mortar onto the concrete base. Also use your trowel to spread mortar onto the sides of the bricks before you bed them down—a technique called "buttering." It takes a bit of practice to butter the right amount onto each brick and to keep the mortar from falling off as you lay each one in place.

3 When the mortar hardens enough so that it's no longer liquid and runny but is still soft and dry enough to press a thumbprint into it, use a jointing tool or wooden dowel to shape a concave depression into each joint. Tool the short joints first, and then the longer joints. Wait a week before cleaning mortar drips or spatters with a stiff brush. (See "Clean the Steps," opposite.)

BRICK STEPS

IN LAYING OUT YOUR STEPS, consider the size of the bricks so that each tread will be made of whole units. The illustration at right shows four different ways of creating brick risers and treads: using different brick thicknesses (1½ or 2¼ inches); laying the bricks flat; setting them on edge; and varying the mortar-joint thickness (⅜ to ½ inch). These options give you some flexibility in achieving the exact height you will need for the risers so that they will add up to the correct overall height. The exposed length of the brick shown produces a tread of 12 inches.

Tread Design. A tread width that is a multiple of 8 inches will accommodate the use of whole bricks. (Two 3⅜-inch-wide bricks laid flat plus two ⅜-inch mortar joints equals 8 inches.) If you draw a plan of the treads, you will be able to calculate the number of paving bricks you'll need.

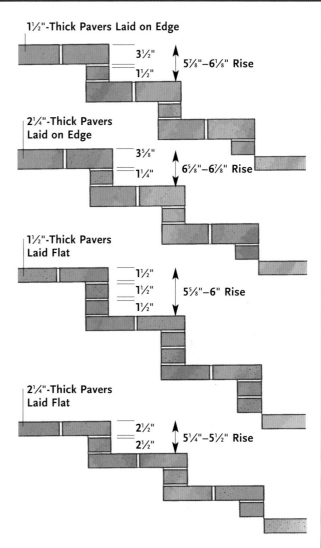

1½"-Thick Pavers Laid on Edge
3½"
1½"
5⅞"–6⅛" Rise

2¼"-Thick Pavers Laid on Edge
3⅝"
1¼"
6⅛"–6⅞" Rise

1½"-Thick Pavers Laid Flat
1½"
1½"
1½"
5⅝"–6" Rise

2¼"-Thick Pavers Laid Flat
2½"
2½"
5¼"–5½" Rise

CLEAN THE STEPS

AFTER THE STEPS HAVE SET for about a week, brush the surface with a stiff natural- or synthetic-bristle brush—or a wire brush—to remove mortar drips and dust. Use a plastic or wooden scraper and a brush to remove large mortar splatters.

If necessary, clean the completed project with a diluted solution of muriatic acid (mixed 1:10 with water). Don't use muriatic acid on white, cream, buff, gray, or brown brick, because it can leave ugly green or brown stains. Before applying an acidic cleaning solution, thoroughly wet the pavers with a garden hose. Wearing rubber gloves, apply the acid solution carefully with a special acid brush (made with polystyrene bristles, available from masonry suppliers). Scrub lightly; then rinse thoroughly with a garden hose. Be extremely careful when working with acid to avoid burns. Don't use metal tools or buckets, because the acid will corrode them. Use plastic. To avoid dangerous splashes, always pour the water in the bucket first, and then add the acid to the water.

soft-set patios 8

A WELL-DESIGNED PATIO often adds more to the value of a home than it costs to build. Patios can range from a simple pad outside a door to a large expanse wrapping around a corner of the house. Typically, patios are about one-third the size of the house. That's larger than most interior rooms. Always consider the terrain when you site a patio, in order to protect it from the hottest sun and coldest wind. Patios should be well drained and built an inch or so above ground level. They should also slope away from the house at a rate of ¼ inch per foot and meet the house 1 to 3 inches below the ground-floor level.

131

SOFT-SET BASICS

Patios are much like walks in that you can lay them over one of two kinds of bases. The simplest is a sand-and-gravel base, which will support flagstone, brick, or interlocking pavers. Mortared brick and stone patios, on the other hand, sit in a mortar bed on top of a concrete pad laid slightly below grade.

The easiest patio you can build uses concrete pavers, brick, flagstone, or adobe block laid on a sand-and-gravel base. Pavers and flagstones of various sizes, shapes, colors, and textures come in a variety of patterns, but anything thinner than 1¼ inches may crack with use. The secret of success in dry-laid paving is a proper base, which minimizes settlement. The base consists of a 4-inch layer of gravel, topped with an easy-to-smooth sand layer. On poorly drained soils and in very cold climates, the drainage base should be 6 inches thick. In some soils and in areas where the ground does not freeze and thaw, you may be able to do without the gravel entirely. Check with your local building office.

Edging. Edging holds the patio surface in place and keeps the individual pavers from moving. If the patio is built at ground level, the earth can serve as an edging. But to discourage flooding, you may want to build your patio slightly higher than grade and put an edging around it. You have your choice of picking an edging that blends with the patio or one that complements the patio material.

Stone slabs that have "natural" joints, opposite, make a unique design statement.

Brick is a classic. Set in a herringbone pattern on a sand-and-gravel base, above, bricks are always a favorite for patios.

Cut flagstones come together in a subtle pattern of various colors and shapes on this spacious patio, left.

Patio pavers laid over a sand-and-gravel base gave the homeowners a lot of value for very little maintenance. Packing the soil underneath them tightly helps to keep the surface smooth.

INSTALLING PATIO PAVERS

Concrete pavers, available at home-improvement centers, can be used to make a simple, attractive patio. Pavers usually have a tab system that helps you space the blocks accurately without measuring. Concrete pavers are available in a variety of patterns, and installation will vary slightly from brand to brand and pattern to pattern. All concrete paving blocks, however, can be laid over a sand-and-gravel bed.

Lay Out the Patio. Use wood 1x2 stakes and string lines to outline your patio. Begin by driving two stakes near the house wall at the patio edges. Set up batter boards at the outer corners. Stretch mason's twine along what will be the perimeter of your patio. (Mason's twine stretches less than string.) Level the twine by hanging a line level at midspan.

Check to make sure the layout is square using the 3-4-5 method described in Chapter 11, page 168. Measure from one stake 3 feet along the house, and then 4 feet along the line. The corner is square when the diagonal between the two points measures 5 feet. If the corner is not square, slide the string along the batter boards until it is, and mark the location of the string on the board. For large areas, increase the measurements proportionally. For example, increase the measurements to 6, 8, and 10 feet.

Square the second line that meets the house; then square the remaining side of the patio.

When all the sides are placed properly, make a saw cut where each string line crosses its batter board. If you need to remove the strings during subsequent work, you can pop them back in the cuts without having to remeasure.

Predominantly red pavers complement the green lushness surrounding this patio. To make way for it, trees were cleared and the ground had to be made level.

PATIO PAVERS ON A SAND BASE

To drain well, the patio should slope away from the house ¼ inch per foot. Adjust your level string lines to reflect this. Then sprinkle sand or flour over the strings to transfer the patio layout to the ground. Where the strings cross to mark the corner of the patio, suspend a plumb bob from the line, and mark the corner with a nail struck through a piece of paper into the ground.

TOOLS & MATERIALS

▌ Work gloves ▌ Safety glasses ▌ String
▌ Line level ▌ Square garden spade ▌ Tamper
▌ Screed board ▌ Gravel ▌ Landscape fabric
▌ Edging material ▌ Sand ▌ Mallet
▌ 1½-in.-diameter pipe ▌ Pavers ▌ 4-ft. level
▌ Circular saw with carbide masonry blade
▌ Stiff-bristle broom ▌ Garden hose

1 If you are working over a lawn, use a square garden spade to cut and remove the sod layer; roll up the sod for reuse in other areas of the yard. Excavate the patio area to the desired depth, including the thickness of the patio paving material and gravel base. Tamp down and level the soil. If you want to discourage weed growth, cover the bare earth with landscape fabric.

2 Add a 4- to 6-in. layer of gravel, and use a garden rake to spread and extend it about 1 ft. beyond the edges on all sides. Different types of gravel are available; sharp-edged gravels, such as granite and bluestone, are preferred as a base because they compress better than smooth gravels, such as pea and river stone. Tamp the gravel well, using a hand or mechanical tamper.

3 Spread landscape fabric over the gravel. This fabric is available in 3 to 4 ft. rolls, which are easy to handle when working alone, or in 8 to 12 ft. rolls, which can cover an entire area with a single sheet. If you use smaller rolls, be sure to overlap the seams by at least 6 in. It is not necessary to pin the fabric; a few shovels of gravel will hold it in place. Continued on next page.

Continued from previous page.

4 Install the edging. This patio will have a plastic edging, but bricks, cobblestones, or lengths of cut stone set on edge are other options. Dig a deeper trench around the perimeter, as needed, to hold the edging. Measure periodically to make sure the trench will put the edging at the desired height. Set it flush with or slightly below what will be the patio's surface.

5 Spread a thin layer of fine sand over the gravel base; then spread coarse concrete sand over the gravel to create a layer that is 1½ in. deep. Use the back edge of a garden rake to smooth the sand in place without disturbing the landscape fabric underneath it. The sand will provide a soft but firm bed for the pavers.

8 To trim a small paver, clamp it to a worktable and cut it using a carbide masonry blade mounted in a circular saw. You can also use a power wet saw to make this cut. A wet saw can be economically rented from a home center or local hardware store by the day or job. It makes smooth, dust-free cuts even in thick, hard stone or concrete masonry paving units.

9 When all the pavers are in place, use a rubber mallet and a 2x4 block to ensure that all of them are seated properly. A mechanical power tamper can also be used and is especially handy when working over large areas. If individual pavers or sections sink or form depressions, pry up the pavers and add sand to bring them back up to the desired level.

6 Push 1½-in.-diameter pipes into the sand along the edges of the patio at the proper grade. Then drag a 2x4 across the pipes to level the bed. If you are working alone or prefer to build your patio in stages, place the pipes about 3 ft. apart. If you have a helper and can manage a longer screed board, lay the pipes up to 8 ft. apart to work large areas quickly and efficiently.

7 Remove the pipes. Then, starting in a corner, begin placing the pavers carefully on the sand. Do not press or twist the pavers into the sand bed. Seat each paver unit with a light tap of a rubber mallet. If you're working with pavers that don't have built-in spacers, position them to create ⅟₁₆- to ⅛-in. joints. Use a level to frequently check that the pavers are even and level.

10 Use a stiff broom to brush dry mortar sand into the joints between pavers. Most pavers have small bumps or lugs formed into their sides that automatically provide the proper spacing from one paver to the next. Packing the joints completely is critical to the integrity of the patio over time. Brush the sand in all directions to ensure even coverage.

11 Thoroughly wet down the patio using a fine mist from a garden hose. Be careful not to spray directly into the joints and dislodge the sand. As the water settles the sand, voids will probably appear. Simply add additional dry sand, and continue to brush it into the joints. Repeat this process as many times as necessary until all of the joints are filled.

mortar-bed patios 9

CONCRETE IS THE MATERIAL builders usually turn to when it comes to constructing permanent patios. Long before wood decks became popular, homes typically had concrete patios that served as outdoor living spaces. Concrete is reasonably easy to work with and forms a hard, stone-like, long-lasting surface that requires little maintenance. You can opt for an all-concrete patio where the concrete serves as the finished surface, or cover the concrete with a more decorative paving material, such as brick, stone, or tile.

CONCRETE PATIOS

For a small patio—80 square feet or less—you can buy a prepackaged concrete mix and mix it in a wheelbarrow. For a larger patio, you can purchase the separate ingredients—portland cement, sand, and gravel—and mix them yourself. Perhaps the most practical method is to have ready-mix concrete delivered by truck to the job site. Ready-mix is sold by the cubic yard, and every 100 square feet of 4-inch-thick patio requires roughly 1.23 cubic yards. A 450-square-foot patio would require 4.5 x 1.23 cubic yards—just over 5½ cubic yards of ready-mix. Add 10 percent for spillage.

Consider ordering air-entrained mix. Air-entrained concrete contains billions of microscopic air bubbles in the hardened slab that act as safety valves to prevent damage caused by freezing and thawing.

Exposed-aggregate concrete has a slightly rough texture that suits an outdoor application. You can usually select the color and type of aggregate to suit your style.

WORKING WITH READY-MIX CONCRETE

TO ORDER READY-MIX, call your dealer at least a day ahead of time. Tell him when you want delivery—the day, time, place, and number of cubic yards. Tell the supplier exactly what you're using the concrete for, so you'll get the right mix. Typically, you'll want a mix with:

- ¾-inch maximum-size coarse aggregate (stones).
- A minimum of six 94-pound bags of portland cement in each cubic yard—for good finishing.
- A maximum slump of 5 inches for hand methods of finishing—slump is a measure of workability.
- From 5 to 7 percent entrained air by volume in a severe climate, and from 3 to 4½ percent in a nonfreezing climate—to aid in finishing.
- A 28-day compressive strength of at least 4,000 pounds per square inch (psi). Compressive strength is a good measure of the strength and durability you'll have in the hardened concrete; a 3,500-psi compressive strength is sufficient for a nonfreezing climate. Check the local building department for recommendations.

If you order ready-mix this way, it should arrive ready to use without adding any water to make it workable. In fact, you should avoid adding water, as that cuts down on the strength and durability of your patio.

If the truck mixer cannot safely back up and dump into your patio forms, you can have the ready-mix pumped through a hose to the construction site. The hose can be routed through a gate, over a fence, or wherever necessary to reach from street to patio. If you think you'll need to have the concrete pumped to the site, be sure to discuss this with the supplier.

On concreting day, have two or more strong helpers on hand when the truck mixer arrives. If the ready-mix will be brought in from the street by wheelbarrow, have an additional two helpers to man the wheelbarrows. Each worker should have work gloves and eye protection. At least one worker—who may have to wade into the mix while placing it—will need rubber boots. Once the concrete is poured, you'll need time to screed (flatten) it and to work the surface several times to create the finish you desire.

Rough-cut slate tiles have been set in mortar on this patio. Their slightly unrefined look suits the Old World decorative theme set by the patio's furnishings.

A natural-stone tile may not always be uniform in size, shape, and particularly, color. If that's important to you, consider a precast concrete-tile look-alike.

BUILDING A CONCRETE PATIO

Building a concrete patio is much like building a concrete walk. Lay out the perimeter of the patio by stretching strings from stakes driven at the house to batter boards at the far end of the patio. Make sure the layout is square using the 3-4-5 triangle method. (See "Using the 3-4-5 Method," page 168.) The patio needs to slope ¼ inch per foot for drainage. Use a line level to get the proper slope.

TOOLS & MATERIALS

- Line level ▪ Stakes ▪ Work gloves
- Pry bar (optional) ▪ Wheelbarrow ▪ Gravel
- Rake ▪ Lumber for forms ▪ Screed
- Power drill-driver ▪ Tamper ▪ Concrete mix
- Welded-wire mesh ▪ Bull float
- Edging and jointing trowels ▪ Burlap

1 Begin by marking off, and then excavating, the patio area. The depth of the excavation will equal the thickness of the slab plus a 4- to 6-in.-deep gravel base. Drive a stake, and measure up from the bottom of the excavation to mark the finished slab surface. Slabs should be pitched slightly to shed water. Use a string and line level to adjust the slope.

4 Concrete is heavy, and it exerts considerable pressure when poured. Build sturdy 2x4 forms to hold the wet concrete. This provides a slab depth of 3½ in., which is adequate for a small slab in most areas. For larger, thicker slabs, use 2x6 forms and pour to the depth desired. Set your stakes below the form board tops to allow clearance for screeding.

5 Use a straight 2x4 to level to screed the gravel. The gravel surface should be no higher than the bottom of the form boards to ensure an even, continuous depth for the concrete pour. Some gravel will extend under and past the forms, which provides a wide, firm footing for the slab and allows any groundwater to disperse from beneath the slab.

2 Prepare the base by leveling the excavated area. Tamp the soil, and remove any large rocks with a pry bar. Small stones do not pose a problem, but over time rocks several inches in diameter or larger can be forced to the surface by groundwater or by freeze-thaw cycles in colder areas. This movement can gradually lift a slab and cause it to crack.

3 Place 4 to 6 in. of crushed stone or gravel over the entire patio area, and use a rake to level and smooth it. The more gravel under the slab, the more it will be protected from ground movement and water. Spaces within the gravel allow groundwater to infill and expand in freezing weather, reducing the buildup of hydrostatic pressure beneath the slab.

6 Tamp the gravel well to ensure a firm, solid base. Using a gas-powered tamper, which can be rented for the day or the job, makes this work go quickly and results in an even, well-compacted surface. Crushed-stone gravel, like that used here, compacts better than round, smooth pea or river gravels and provides a solid base for the heavy concrete.

7 After compacting the gravel, cover the entire slab area with wire reinforcing mesh. Several mesh types and sizes are available. For poured concrete slabs, masons typically specify 6 x 6-in. uncoated wire mesh. The mesh helps to prevent cracking as the concrete shrinks and expands. Overlap mesh sections by 6 in., and tie them together with wire. Continued on next page.

Continued from previous page.

8 Place boards for wheelbarrow ramps to prevent collapsing the forms as the concrete is delivered to the site. When you begin pouring the wet concrete mix, dump each load against the previous one. Place blocks under the mesh, or use a rake to lift the mesh into the middle of the slab. Use a hoe to spread the mix evenly, and fill to just above the forms.

9 Slice into the concrete mix with a shovel or trowel to eliminate air pockets and voids, especially along the form edges and in corners. Shovel the concrete into low spots—screeding is easier if the forms are slightly overfull. With a helper at one end, push and pull a straight 2x4 screed board along the top of the forms to level the still-wet concrete.

12 While the concrete is still uncured—just as it begins to stiffen up—run an edging tool along the entire perimeter of the pour. Insert the tool between the form and slab, and use light pressure to pull it in a continuous sweep along the edges. This will round the edges, which helps to strengthen them and makes them less brittle or prone to chipping.

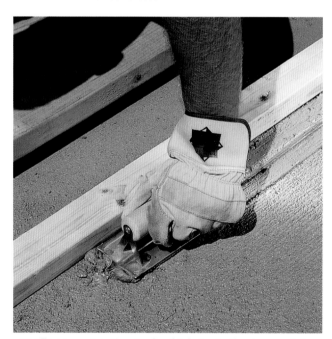

13 Use a jointing tool, which is similar to an edging tool, to create control joints in the slab. Concrete shrinks as its moisture dries and the mix hardens, and cracks may occur for a variety of reasons. Control joints spaced at recommended intervals may not prevent slabs from cracking, but they will stop cracks from spreading or continuing into adjacent areas.

10 Use a long wood darby or a bull float attached to an extension pole, as shown, to level the screeded concrete. Floating helps to force the aggregate in the mix below the concrete surface. As you work the darby or float across the surface with a swirling motion, keep the leading edges slightly raised to avoid digging into the wet "mud."

11 Concrete surfaces can be easily finished to a puttylike smoothess, but outdoor patios need a more textured surface to prevent them from becoming slick when wet, making walking hazardous. Give the surface some "tooth" by going over the uncured slab with a stiff broom. One light pass of the broom in each direction is usually all that is needed.

14 When the concrete dries hard enough so that you can't see an impression when you step on it, mist the entire surface with a fine spray of clean water, and cover the slab with burlap or polyethylene sheeting to keep it from drying out. Concrete takes about a month to fully harden. Keeping it moist while it cures, or hydrates, is critical to the process.

15 As concrete hardens, it develops most of its strength within the first week or so. Cure the slab for at least five to seven days, or longer if possible, before walking on it or placing heavy objects on it. Mist the surface periodically to keep it damp, and keep a covering in place to help retain the moisture. Spray-on compounds to hasten curing are also available.

PATTERNED-CONCRETE SYSTEMS

ALTHOUGH NOT A DO-IT-YOURSELF PROJECT, patterned concrete (some companies refer to the process as stamping, stenciling, or texturing) provides a good way to get the look of natural stone or brick while using concrete. Some samples are shown here, but for a wider selection, check the manufacturers in the resource guide.

PATIOS ON CONCRETE SLABS

The most elegant-looking patios are made of flagstone, brick, or tile, and are mortared together. These patios wear and weather well, and are quite durable. Like mortared walks, mortared patios sit on a concrete slab to provide support and prevent cracking. Pouring a slab and applying the brick, stone, or tile is a serious time commitment. You can often shortcut the process by applying stone or brick over an existing concrete patio. To build a stone or brick patio from the ground up, pour a slab as described in "Building a Concrete Patio," page 146. Dig and lay the base so that pad elevation will place the pavers at the desired height. Then follow the directions opposite.

COVERING AN EXISTING PATIO

THE CONCRETE BASE SLAB may be new or old, but it must be clean, sound, and free of oil, grease, and loose materials, such as dust, paint, and efflorescence. Clean the slab thoroughly with a solution of 1 part muriatic acid to 9 parts water. This is a strong acid: for safety's sake, pour the water first; then the acid. Wear heavy rubber gloves, long sleeves, goggles, and a vapor respirator. Apply the solution with a stiff-bristle brush. Rinse thoroughly with clean water.

A scaled surface that is structurally sound presents no problem because the new surface will cover it. If the slab has settled unevenly, in most cases it can be corrected by installing the units on a thick, corrective layer of mortar. Every crack and joint in the old slab, however, must coincide with a joint in the new paving. Otherwise, movement across the crack or joint will damage the new paving.

Cover all joints and cracks in the base slab with something to hold the mortar—½- by ½-inch sticky-back weather stripping will work. Follow the cracks faithfully.

Paving raises the elevation of a slab—make sure you have room for what you're planning. It wouldn't do to have your patio end up higher than the house floor, for example. In fact, to prevent flooding, make sure that there is at least a 1-inch drop from the threshold to the new patio surface.

TILING A PATIO

project

If you're using an existing slab, it should be structurally sound and free of oil and waxy films and foreign matter. The slab should be properly sloped, well drained, suitably flat, and not subject to dampness from beneath. If the surface has been troweled, be sure to coat it with a concrete bonder.

TOOLS & MATERIALS

▌Tools needed for concrete slab if necessary
▌Work gloves ▌Chalk-line box ▌Tile
▌Notched trowel ▌Thinset adhesive
▌Plastic spacers ▌Tile cutters
▌Mallet ▌Plastic sheeting
▌Backer rod if necessary ▌Grout
▌Exterior-grade caulk ▌Rubber float
▌Sponge ▌Tile sealer

1 Tiles used for outdoor patios must be approved for exterior use. Choose tiles that will not absorb water or be slippery when wet. If tiling over an existing slab, the concrete must be clean and structurally sound. Begin your layout by snapping chalk lines across the length and width of the slab. Do a dry run, and adjust the tile layout to minimize cuts.

2 Thinset mortar, sold by the bag, is easy to mix and apply. Smooth and free of aggregates, it can fill minor depressions or chips in the slab as it is applied, but large depressions must be patched beforehand. Spread thinset mortar with a notched trowel. Hold the trowel at an angle, and rake the mortar to the proper depth for setting the tiles.

3 Apply mortar up to the chalk lines, but keep the lines visible to guide your layout. Spread the thinset over an area about 3 to 4 ft. square, or sufficient to allow you to place tiles without disturbing any tiles already set in the mortar. Begin in the center of the layout, and set the field tiles first. Border tiles are cut and installed last.

Continued on next page.

Mortar-Bed Patios

Continued from previous page.

4 As you set each tile in place, insert plastic spacers to keep the tiles evenly separated and your layout square to your chalk lines. You can remove the spacers after the mortar sets or leave them in place and grout over them if you have set them deep enough. Use a snap cutter or wet saw to cut the border tiles if necessary. Seat each tile with light taps from a rubber mallet.

5 You should install floor or patio tiles square to the layout grid; however, the existing house walls or slab edges may not be square. In that case, measure and cut border tiles individually to compensate for any slight variations where they meet obstacles. Leave a joint space of ½ in. or less along edges, which you can grout or cover with trim.

8 Use a high-quality, exterior-grade caulk to fill all perimeter joints. Be sure to fill the joints to above grade. Choose a caulk that will remain flexible in cold weather and resists shrinking as it ages. Caulks are available in a wide range of colors to match house siding or foundation walls, and some products may be mixed and colored to suit your needs.

9 After the thinset has had adequate time to harden, remove the plastic sheeting and pry out any loose or raised tile spacers. Vacuum the joints thoroughly to remove all loose material. Mix tile grout to a thin, but not watery, consistency; then apply it with a rubber float. Work diagonally across the joints, pressing the grout into the spaces between tiles.

6 After setting the tiles, cover them with plastic sheeting and allow the mortar to cure, usually 24 to 48 hours. If the patio is in full sun or you have installed it during very hot weather, spray a light mist of water over the installation before placing the sheeting to keep the thinset damp. Do not allow water to pool, however—too much water will weaken the mortar as it sets.

7 To prevent rainwater, snowmelt, or insects from entering the vulnerable joint between the house and patio, stuff the joint with closed-cell foam backer rod, which is available in several diameters. Be sure to fill any opening larger than ¼ in. around the perimeter of the patio. Press the filler into the joint to allow room for a top layer of waterproof caulk.

10 Let the grout set for about 15 minutes; then wipe any excess off the face of the tiles using a damp sponge. Again, work diagonally across the joints, being careful not to dislodge the grout. Avoid over-wetting the grout. As the tiles dry, a thin haze may form on the surface; use a soft, clean cloth to wipe off this haze and polish the entire patio.

11 Keep the patio damp and re-cover it with plastic sheeting for up to one week. After the grout cures, apply a tile sealer with a sponge, pad, or roller. Apply two to three initial coats, following the product directions. Also follow the manufacturer's application schedule for reapplying the sealer at regular intervals to maintain its exterior protection.

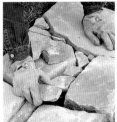

dry-laid stone walls 10

STONEWORK IS A CRAFT that requires little more than a strong back and some patience. Most of it doesn't call for specialized skills or tools—it's just plain hard work. As long as you are prepared for the physical effort and the mental challenge of putting together what is, in effect, a three-dimensional jigsaw puzzle in stone, building a stone wall can be an enjoyable and rewarding project.

WHAT YOU NEED

A dry-laid stone wall is the simplest of masonry jobs. No footing is required (as long as the wall is less than 3 feet high), and you won't have to mix mortar or fuss with joints. Walls laid 100 years ago are still standing in excellent shape, so a dry-laid wall can be a beautiful and permanent part of your landscape.

Tools

The tools you'll need are elementary. Get a measuring tape, a sharp-bladed shovel, a pickax for removing stones in the way of the wall, and a stonemason's hammer and chisel. Stakes, string, a mason's level, and a site-made batter gauge will aid in laying out and stacking the wall.

A prybar comes in handy for moving stones. Wear heavy leather gloves for handling stones and safety glasses when splitting them. Stone walls more than 3 feet high may require special techniques, however, so it's best to leave their construction to an experienced stonemason.

Selecting Stones

Whether you buy stones or scrounge for them, choose ones that have flat sides and edges. This is especially important if you're building a dry-laid wall, because the only thing holding each stone in place is its weight.

Select stones with at least three flat sides—the top, bottom, and one side—to use for the face of the wall. Avoid large egg-shaped or round stones, but make sure you have a good variety of sizes and shapes to provide the best design and construction.

Walls look best if they contain a good mixture of large and small stones of different colors, set randomly over the entire surface. Set small stones around large ones, and avoid grouping too many of a single size or color in one area of the wall.

Although the project will go faster if you use large stones, you must be able to move them easily—make sure they aren't too large or heavy to lift. Generally, it's easy to work with stones that weigh from 15 to 30 pounds, and they'll be in scale with most backyard garden projects.

A dry-laid stone wall can endure with little maintenance for many years.

smart tip

MAKE A BATTER GAUGE

Stone walls should slope inward from bottom to top. To check inward slope, use a batter, or slope gauge, with a level. Make the gauge from 1x2s joined at one end and spread apart at the other. The difference between the two ends is the slope you want to maintain. The level should read plumb when held against the wall.

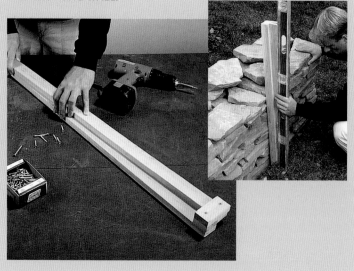

TYPES OF STONE

STONES USED FOR WALL CONSTRUCTION can be divided into two broad categories: rubble and cut stone. Generally, the exact kinds of stone are limited to the types found in your area. Stones sold at masonry and patio supply houses and at stone yards can be expensive. You may save money by looking elsewhere. Stones from road-construction sites, local farms, building-demolition sites, and landscape-remodeling projects may be free for the hauling. Also check the classified section of the newspaper.

If you decide to scrounge for your own stones, you'll need a sturdy pickup truck or a trailer with good springs and tires to haul away the rock. It doesn't take many stones to add up to a ton, so you may find yourself making more trips than anticipated. When budgeting, factor in your time, gasoline, and wear-and-tear on your vehicle.

Rubble and Fieldstone. Rubble consists of irregularly shaped stones. These are the stones that are often blasted or bulldozed from road-construction sites or they can be pieces left over from stones that have be cut or trimmed at a quarry. Rubble is usually the least-expensive stone you can buy.

Fieldstones generally have rounded edges as a result of glacial or water action. As the name implies, some of these stones are taken from plowed fields. Others are from alongside a creek or a river.

Cut Stone. Also referred to as quarried stone, cut stone is available semidressed or fully dressed from stone yards and landscape suppliers. Semidressed stones, such as cobblestones, are roughly square with smooth sides and uniform thickness. Fully dressed stones, called "ashlar," are trimmed to precise rectangular shapes.

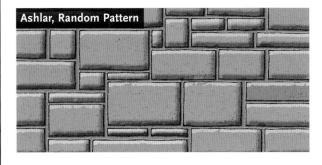

Rubble, Mortared

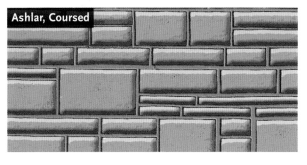

Rubble, Dry-Laid

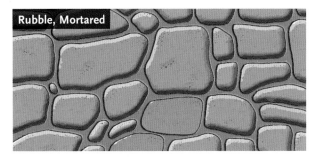

Cut Stone, Random Placement

Cut Stone, Coursed

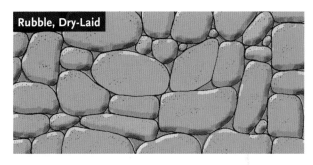

Ashlar, Random Pattern

Ashlar, Coursed

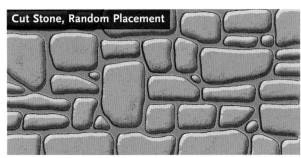

Irregularly shaped stones in many sizes and colors reflect the variety in nature, which makes this patio blend so well with its setting.

Dry-Laid Stone Walls

Estimating Amounts

Stone is sold by the cubic yard or by the ton. To estimate how much you'll need for your wall, multiply the width by the length by the height—all measured in feet. Divide this number by 27. It's a good idea to order an extra 10 percent to compensate for breakage. If the stone is sold by the ton, have the stone dealer determine the number of tons needed for your wall project.

If you're scrounging your own rubble or fieldstone, simply measure the volume of each truckload, and then divide this figure into the volume of the wall to determine the number of loads needed. Allow 25 percent extra to compensate for voids between the stones, which have been tossed randomly in the truck.

When you get the stones home, sort them by size into different groups near the construction site. First find flat stones wide enough to span the full thickness of the wall. You'll put these stones every 4 to 6 feet in the wall to tie together the two parallel rows that make up the front and back of the wall. Place these stones, called "bond stones," near where you will use them. Then find other stones with straight edges and sides for the ends or corners of the wall. Place these stones near where you will lay them, as well. It's best to spread the end and bond stones in groups that are one layer thick and about 4 to 6 feet away from the proposed base so that you can spot any stone you need.

Built into a hillside, a dry-laid stone wall offers opportunities for attractive landscaping that might include a water feature in addition to plantings.

WALL-BUILDING BASICS

DRY-LAID STONE WALLS lend a rustic appearance to the landscape, and they are easy to build once you develop an eye for picking the right stones and fitting them together. A dry-laid stone wall makes a good low retaining wall; the spaces between the stones prevent water from building up behind the wall, as can sometimes happen with a mortared wall.

Building Requirements. A freestanding dry-laid wall can be straight or can have corners, curves, or any combination of these. Because the wall is held together by nothing more than gravity, your main goal is to avoid building a wall that is top heavy.

A rule of thumb is that a wall up to 3 feet high must be at least 2 feet wide. Freestanding walls more than 2 feet high generally have a slight inward slope, or batter, from the bottom to the top. Battered-wall faces lean against each other, holding the stones in place. Walls up to 3 feet high should have 1 inch of batter for each 2 feet of rise, although a wall 2 feet or less can be built with a plumb face. (For help in determining the correct batter, see "Make a Batter Gauge," on page 156.)

Footings. Dry-laid walls less than 3 feet high usually require no footings. If the soil is firm, you can lay the stones directly on the ground. For the best appearance and stability, lay the first course of stones below grade.

Bond Patterns. Freestanding stone walls are typically stacked two stones thick. These parallel face courses are called "wythes." To tie the wythes together, bond stones are placed at each end of the wall and at 4- to 6-foot intervals in each course of the wall. Usually, the more bond stones you can incorporate into the wall, the stronger it will be. As you build each successive course, stagger the joints so that each stone rests on at least two stones beneath it. Gaps can be filled with small rubble stones.

Dry-Laid Stone Walls

BUILDING THE WALL

project

Have a helper or two on hand when you're lifting heavy stones into position. After deciding on the location and the length of the wall, drive temporary stakes into the ground to mark the ends of the wall. Stretch a mason's line between the stakes to mark the sides of the wall. You can also place a line level on the string and use it as a guide for keeping the wall level. Dig a trench between the lines. Remove any sod or loose topsoil with a flat-bladed shovel.

TOOLS & MATERIALS

- Work Gloves ▌ Stones ▌ Stakes and string
- Shovel ▌ Garden trowel ▌ Hammer
- Spirit level or batter gauge
- Shims or wedges ▌ Mortar mix and box
- Mason's trowel ▌ Hawk ▌ Cap stones

1 Sort the stones, grouping them by size before you begin building. Do this near, but not in the way of, your wall location to avoid having to move the stones more than necessary. Set aside the flattest stones for the first course. This will give you a solid, fairly level base to start and will help you establish the proper shape and angle for the wall.

2 Dig into the soil to create a shallow trench slightly wider than your intended wall to provide a smooth, flat base for the first course of stones. The trench should be about as deep as your first course of stones. Try not to disturb the soil below this level to maintain a firm earthen foundation, which the weight of the stacked stones will not compact over time.

3 At each end of the wall, place a flat, double-width stone that spans both rows. This "bond" stone will help to establish a strong, unified corner across the width of the wall that bridges and ties together the alternating base stones. When ordering stone, make sure your supplier provides a sufficient number of large stones to span the wall's full width. Continued on next page.

Continued from previous page.

4 Dry-laid walls are meant to be irregular, but that does not mean they should not be straight or sloppily constructed. Stretch a string line or use a wood straightedge (removed for clarity) as a temporary guide for your first course, and lay the stones up to this guide along the outside edge of the wall. Be selective as you choose the stones, and place irregular edges inward.

5 Slope the base stones slightly inward to establish the wall's angled vertical face, or "batter." This creates a stronger wall because the weight of the stones will cause them to press against one another, and they will be less likely to shift or fall outward as they slowly settle into place. Fill interior gaps between larger stones with smaller stones and rubble.

8 Dry-laid stone walls should slope inward slightly for stability. Use a level to check your work, or construct a batter gauge that enables you to maintain a consistent angle as you proceed upward. Estimate about 1 in. of batter for every 2 ft. of wall height. In general, walls less than 2 ft. tall do not require batter and can be vertically plumb.

9 As you work, prop up larger stones by using small ones as wedges. Be sure to fill the gaps as tightly as possible to avoid a loose-jointed wall, especially if the wall will be more than 1 or 2 ft. high. When it's necessary, use a mason's hammer to chip away any projections or angles that cause larger stones to rock after you've placed them in position.

6 As you continue to stack the stones, occasionally span the width of the wall using a double-wide stone to strengthen and to tie together alternating stones. The general rule for wall-building is "one over two, two over one." This prevents weak joints and joints that extend between rows, and it applies to both horizontal runs and vertical stacking.

7 In alternating courses at the ends of the wall, install square-edged cross stones, as you did at the base corners. Note how smaller stones can be fitted together to fill in behind a larger stone. Constructing a dry-laid wall is like putting together a three-dimensional jigsaw puzzle, a process that takes time and patience as well as physical strength.

10 To ensure that cap stones remain in place and for safety as well as stability, trowel a 1- to 2-in.-thick bed of mortar over the top courses. This will help to level the area and form a base for the cap stones. Uniformly shaped or cut stones are best for this. You can choose stone that complements the wall or provides contrast in type or color.

11 Bed the cap stones into the mortar, pressing them in place with light pressure so that the mortar does not squeeze out from under them. If you have stones cut for this application, order them to a size that overhangs the wall slightly. As an alternative to cap stones, you can finish a wall with a bed of mortar that's 2 to 4 in. thick and crowned in the center.

wall foundations 11

A MORTARED WALL IS RIGID. Unfortunately, the ground below it isn't. As a result, mortared walls require a base of concrete, or footing, beneath them. Without a footing, a wall is at the mercy of the soil, which may not offer enough support or stability to keep the wall from sinking, cracking, or collapsing. A concrete footing spreads the weight of the wall over the soil, bridges soft spots that can cause a wall to crack, and provides support as the soil settles or moves.

Wall Foundations

FOUNDATION FUNDAMENTALS

The size of the footing and the way you will construct it will depend on a few factors—your climate, your property's soil conditions, and the height and weight of the wall the footings must support. Building codes are very specific regarding footing requirements, so be sure to check with your local building department before you finalize your plans—and certainly before you begin construction.

Footing Size and Depth

As a rule of thumb, footing width should be either twice the width or two thirds the height of the wall, whichever is greater. If you plan to build a brick wall that incorporates pilasters into the design, make sure the footing follows

BUYING CONCRETE

CONCRETE CONSISTS OF A MIXTURE of portland cement, sand, and gravel. Depending on the job and your budget, you can buy bags of premixed concrete and add water; purchase the ingredients and mix your own; or have a wet-concrete mix delivered by truck.

Dry Mixes

Purchasing dry concrete mix in 60- or 80-pound bags may prove convenient for jobs requiring less than ½ cubic yard of concrete. But because it takes about twenty 80-pound sacks to make a ½ cubic yard, larger jobs can be quite expensive and labor intensive. If you use premixed bags, it may be worthwhile to have them delivered. Make sure none of the sacks has already hardened. Be sure to store the concrete somewhere dry and off the ground on something like a pallet.

Mixing Your Own. You can usually save money on jobs requiring more than ½ cubic yard of concrete by buying cement and aggregates separately and mixing them yourself. Cement is sold by the 94-pound sack. (Type I cement is commonly used in residential work. Types II through IV are used in more massive structures.) Masons refer to sand as fine aggregate and gravel as coarse aggregate. Both are sold by the cubic yard. For home use, cement is commonly mixed with bank-run sand, because the round particles make for a stronger mix. For coarse aggregate, use stone or gravel ranging from ½ to 1½ inches in diameter.

All aggregates must be free of silt and debris. To test, place about 2 inches of aggregate in a glass jar. Pour in water, and shake gently. Wait for the water to clear. If there is more than ⅛ inch of silt on top of the aggregate, you'll have to wash it. Simply dump the aggregate on a clean, hard surface, and hose it down.

Wet Mixes

For concrete footings and walls requiring 1 or more cubic yards of concrete, ordering a wet, or transit mix, may be your best bet. The wet concrete can be poured directly into the footings from the truck, saving hours of back-breaking labor. If the truck can't get to within about 20 feet of the forms, the concrete can be pumped from the truck through a hose. This method usually costs extra. A cheaper but more difficult method is to cart the concrete to the forms with a few wheelbarrows and some strong backs.

Air-Entrained Concrete. In cold climates subject to severe freeze and thaw conditions, air-entrained concrete is common. This type of concrete contains millions of tiny air pockets that allow water to freeze and expand without damaging the concrete. The air-entraining agent can be added to Types I, II, and III concrete, but you'll need a power mixer to activate the agent in the mix. Check with your supplier to find out if air-entrained concrete is common in your area.

Estimating Amounts

The amount of concrete required for a footing is the biggest determining factor when deciding how to order concrete. To figure out the amount needed, multiply the footing width by its depth, working in inches. Divide by 144 to get square feet. Then multiply this figure by the overall length of the footing in feet to get cubic feet. To figure cubic yards, divide the number of cubic feet by 27.

The easiest way to determine quantities is to provide a concrete supplier with the footing dimensions and let them compute the amounts of each ingredient and an overall price.

the shape of the wall. Otherwise, make the footing wide enough to accommodate the extra width of the pilasters. As with all masonry walls, the top of the footing should be several inches below ground level so that it won't show once the wall is built.

Footings should be at least 6 inches thick. If frost heave is a problem in your area, you'll have to set the footing below the frost line. Local codes vary regarding the exact depth, so check for standards in your area.

Footing Forms

Forms, usually two-by boards, hold wet concrete to the shape required for the footing. In firm soil that retains its shape after digging, the excavation itself can be the form. In this case, place leveled 2x4s at the top of the excavation.

You'll need the 2x4s as a guide when you level the concrete. For loose soil, use wide boards (2x6s, 2x8s, 2x10s, etc.) that extend the full depth of the footing. Once the concrete hardens, the forms are usually removed.

smart tip

POOR DRAINAGE

IN SOIL WITH POOR DRAINAGE, PLACE THE FOOTING ON A TAMPED GRAVEL BASE AT LEAST 6 INCHES THICK. THE GRAVEL BASE PREVENTS WATER FROM COLLECTING BENEATH THE FOOTING, MINIMIZING SOIL MOVEMENT.

FOOTINGS AND FORMS

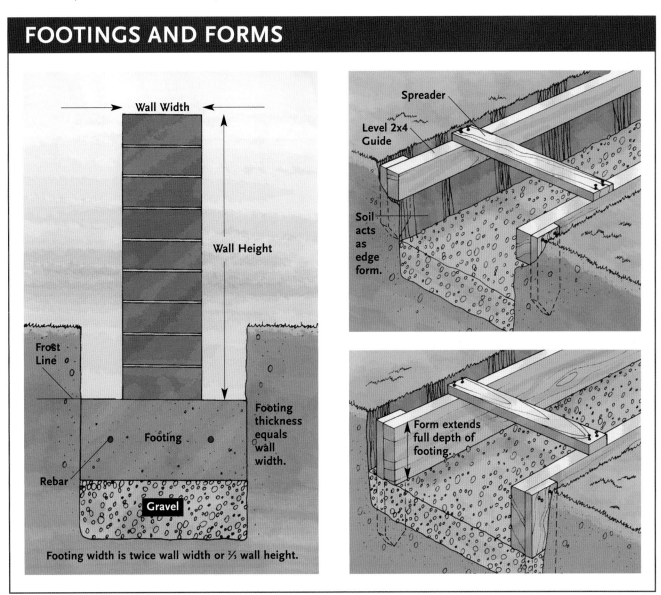

Wall Width

Wall Height

Frost Line

Footing

Rebar

Gravel

Footing thickness equals wall width.

Footing width is twice wall width or ⅔ wall height.

Spreader

Level 2x4 Guide

Soil acts as edge form.

Form extends full depth of footing.

BUILDING FOOTINGS

ONCE YOU'VE ESTABLISHED WHERE to build a wall, use stakes, string, and batter boards to mark the footing location and to guide in digging trenches and positioning forms. If your wall will define property lines, be sure the footing is properly positioned so that you don't have to tear down the wall later.

Layout of Footings. For a straight wall, drive stakes into the ground to mark the four corners. For a wall that turns a corner, drive a stake at each end of the wall and one at the outside corner of the wall.

Measure out 3 to 4 feet beyond each stake, and erect a set of batter boards. The horizontal boards should be at least 1 foot wider than the anticipated width of the footing trench. Align the center of the board with the rough center point of the wall you will construct.

Refer to "Batter Board Layout," below right. Then on the crosspieces, measure your wall's width from the string and mark the other face of the wall (A). Measure to find the edges of the footing (B) and the edges of the footing trench (C); mark them on the

board, too. Remember that the footing width is either twice as wide as the wall or two-thirds the wall height, whichever is greater. The trench itself should be between 1 and 2 feet wider than the footing to provide room for installing the formwork. At each mark, use a handsaw to make shallow cuts in the crosspieces to hold the strings in place.

Building Forms

After you dig the trench, compact the soil in the trench bottom with a hand tamper to prevent settling. Then fill the entire trench bottom with at least 6 inches of gravel.

Install the Stakes. Drive 2x4 stakes at the outside corners of the trench. Stretch string between the corner stakes, and level it with the help of a string level. Use the string as a guide to install intermediate stakes about every 2 feet. If the form boards are long enough to reach between the corner stakes, it may be easier to attach and level the form boards first, and then use them as guides to install the intermediate stakes.

Using the 3-4-5 Method

Here's a method that ensures corners are square. Mark one string tied to a batter board 3 feet from the corner. Mark the other string 4 feet from the corner. Measure the distance between the marks. If it is 5 feet, the corner is square. If it isn't, adjust the string until the distance is correct.

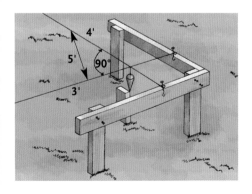

Batter Board Layout

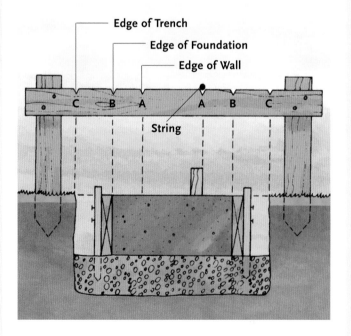

Edge of Trench
Edge of Foundation
Edge of Wall

C B A A B C

String

BUILDING FORMS

project

Many homeowners and builders use screws and a drill-driver to fasten temporary parts, such as spreaders on footing forms. But if you use an old-fashioned hammer, save yourself some time and trouble by driving double-headed nails. After you drive them home, the second head still protrudes, making it easy to pull out the nails as you strip the forms.

TOOLS & MATERIALS

- Work gloves ▌ Measuring tape
- Shovels ▌ Gravel ▌ Tampers
- Lumber for forms ▌ Drill-driver
- Screws ▌ Hammer
- Duplex nails (optional)
- Level ▌ Rebar ▌ Bricks or blocks
- Wire for rebar ▌ Pliers

1 Footings can be placed directly on firm soil, but some codes require forms to be built and a layer of gravel to be spread beneath the footings. An inspection after the footings are poured may also be required. Check with your code officials before you begin. Footing forms don't have to be fancy, however. Secure them with stakes and use plywood gussets where boards meet.

2 Use two-by lumber to build footing forms, and reinforce long, tall, and wide forms with stretchers every 4 to 6 ft. to prevent the boards from spreading. Level the boards as you attach them to the stakes, using guide strings to keep them straight. Use double-headed, or "duplex," nails that can be easily removed, to secure the forms to the stakes.

3 Continuous-length metal reinforcing bars, or rebar, are usually required in footings. Rebar should be positioned about one-third of the way up from the bottom of the forms. To keep the rebar in place as the concrete is poured, prop it up on bricks or other blocks, and check that it stays in place during the pour. Tie lengths of rebar with metal wire.

An undulating row of hedges and a color splash from coral-red roses dress up the low wall that borders this property.

WORKING WITH CONCRETE

Whether you're using a premix or separate ingredients, decide if you want to mix the concrete by hand or rent a power mixer. Weigh the rental costs against the time and effort you'll save by using a power mixer. A power mixer also ensures a more even mix and is a necessity when you're mixing air-entrained concrete.

Mixing by Hand

Hand mixing concrete involves a using square-point shovel, a mason's hoe, or a garden rake to combine the dry concrete ingredients and, subsequently, mix in the water. Hand mixing is hard work. While you can mix the ingredients in a wheelbarrow, it's usually easier to mix them on a clean, flat surface, such as an old sheet of plywood, or in a mortar box, also called "a concrete barge." (See "Mixing Concrete," opposite.)

USING A POWER MIXER

POWER MIXERS COME IN TWO VARIETIES: electrically powered and gas powered. If you rent a gas-powered mixer, have the rental people start the engine to make sure it operates easily. If you use an electric mixer, make sure you can provide electricity to the mixing site. If an extension cord is required, check that the wire gauge is heavy enough to handle the amperage drawn by the motor. If the cord is long, use a wire gauge that is even heavier than required—the available voltage drops as electricity travels along a wire. The rental people can advise you on the appropriate type of cord for the job. Position the mixer as close to the sand and gravel piles as possible.

With the mixer turned off, add the amounts of dry ingredients needed. Measure carefully, and keep track of the amounts so that subsequent batches are consistent. You may need to experiment with different proportions at first. Turn on the mixer, and run it for a few minutes to allow the dry ingredients to mix thoroughly. With the mixer running, pour in a small amount of water, and allow it to blend into the mixture. Continue adding water a little at a time until the mixture reaches the correct consistency. If you're not familiar with this method, it's a good idea to stop the mixer periodically and check the mix, as described above. Once the concrete is mixed, tilt the mixer barrel to pour it into a wheelbarrow for transport to the forms. Have a helper hold the wheelbarrow steady.

CONCRETE INGREDIENTS BY PROPORTION

Maximum Size Coarse Aggregate	AIR-ENTRAINED CONCRETE				CONCRETE WITHOUT AIR			
	Number of Parts per Ingredient				Number of Parts per Ingredient			
	Cement	Sand*	Coarse Aggregate	Water	Cement	Sand*	Coarse Aggregate	Water
$\frac{3}{8}$	1	$2\frac{1}{4}$	$1\frac{1}{2}$	$\frac{1}{2}$	1	$2\frac{1}{2}$	$1\frac{1}{2}$	$1\frac{1}{2}$
$\frac{1}{2}$	1	$2\frac{1}{4}$	2	$\frac{1}{2}$	1	$2\frac{1}{2}$	2	$\frac{1}{2}$
$\frac{3}{4}$	1	$2\frac{1}{4}$	$2\frac{1}{2}$	$\frac{1}{2}$	1	$2\frac{1}{2}$	$2\frac{1}{2}$	$\frac{1}{2}$
1	1	$2\frac{1}{4}$	$2\frac{3}{4}$	$\frac{1}{2}$	1	$2\frac{1}{2}$	$2\frac{3}{4}$	$\frac{1}{2}$
$1\frac{1}{2}$	1	$2\frac{1}{4}$	3	$\frac{1}{2}$	1	$2\frac{1}{2}$	3	$\frac{1}{2}$

Note: 7.48 gallons of water equals 1 cubic foot. One 94-pound bag of portland cement equals about 1 cubic foot.
* "wet" sand sold for most construction use.

The combined finished volume is approximately two-thirds the sum of the original bulk volumes.

MIXING CONCRETE

project

As a rule of thumb, add 6 to 7 gallons of water for every 90-pound bag of cement in the mix. If you use too little water, the concrete won't be fluid enough to fill out the form. Too much water results in weak concrete. Start with 1 or 2 gallons of water, and keep track of the amount you use so that you can add the same amount to subsequent batches.

TOOLS & MATERIALS

- Work gloves ▌Wheelbarrow
- Plywood for mixing surface
- Plywood for measuring box
- Shovel ▌Gravel
- Sand ▌Cement
- Rake ▌Hoe
- Bucket ▌Water

1 Batches of concrete for smaller footings are easily mixed by hand. For footings that require more than 1 cu. yd. of concrete, it's usually more efficient to have it delivered wet by a transit mix provider. To mix your own concrete ingredients, build a measuring box by cutting and assembling five pieces of plywood, each measuring 12 sq. in.

2 In a mortar box or wheelbarrow, or on a large, flat surface such as a sheet of plywood, use a hoe or rake to blend the dry ingredients. Concrete recipes vary, but most include cement, sand, gravel, and water. If you need to mix several batches, use the same amount of ingredients for each batch. Mix all ingredients thoroughly before adding the water.

3 After mixing the dry ingredients, add clean water. This is a critical component, and it must be added in exactly the right proportion or it could easily spoil the mix and weaken the concrete. Add the water in small amounts at a time, blending it into the mix until you reach the proper consistency. Keep track of the amount you add for additional batches.

This mortared wall rests on concrete footings that will keep it stable for many years.

POURING CONCRETE FOR A FOOTING

project

After the formwork is complete, prepare the site for pouring concrete. Make sure you can get the concrete to the forms. Have several helpers with shovels available to spread the concrete in the forms as it is poured. Do not let the concrete mound up in one area.

Allow the concrete to cure for about one week before building the wall. During this time, keep it moist by sprinkling it with water several times a day, then covering it with plastic sheeting. When curing is complete, remove the forms.

TOOLS & MATERIALS

▌Work gloves ▌Motor oil or release agent ▌Brush ▌Shovels ▌Concrete ▌Wheelbarrow ▌Trowels ▌Screed ▌Rebar or bolts

smart tip

TELLING WHEN CONCRETE IS READY

AFTER MIXING, TEST THE CONSISTENCY OF THE CONCRETE BY PLACING A GOOD-SIZE CLUMP ON A CLEAN SURFACE. WORK THE MIXTURE BRIEFLY USING A TROWEL. IF THE MIXTURE IS TOO WET, RIDGES MADE WITH THE TROWEL WON'T HOLD THEIR SHAPE. IF THE MIXTURE IS TOO DRY, YOU WON'T BE ABLE TO MAKE RIDGES AT ALL AS THE CONCRETE WILL FORM DRY LUMPS (BELOW LEFT). WHEN THE MIXTURE IS READY, THE CONCRETE WILL HOLD MOST OF ITS SHAPE AND ONLY A LITTLE WATER WILL BE VISIBLE (BELOW RIGHT).

3 Work the concrete into corners and against the form boards to eliminate all possible voids. It pays to have helpers on hand whenever you work with fresh concrete. Although wet concrete usually has a generous "open" time and does not set up, or harden, too quickly, you have only a limited time to finish it properly before it becomes solid.

1 Prepare the forms for the concrete by brushing motor oil or a release agent on the boards to prevent the concrete from adhering to them. Dampen, but don't soak, the trench and gravel to keep the wet concrete from drying too fast. As the concrete is poured into the forms, use a shovel or hoe to spread it out. Try to pour it evenly in one layer.

2 Using a shovel, slice into the concrete to remove air pockets and distribute the mixture. Tamp the mixture as you go to help settle it in place, but be careful not to disturb any rebar or reinforcing mesh, if you use it. Add concrete as needed in low spots, and overfill the forms slightly to make it easier to later strike off, or screed, the surface smooth.

4 As soon as the forms are filled and ready, strike off the excess poured concrete by working a straight two-by lumber screed across the top of the forms in a back-and-forth motion. Wide footings may require workers on both sides of the forms, pulling a longer board in unison. A level, even surface is all that is required for footings; additional finishing is unnecessary.

5 Install attachment bolts or vertical rebar while the concrete is still wet. Vertical rebar is typically used for hollow concrete-block walls or double-wythe brick walls. You can install short rebar stubs without support and tie in additional lengths later. If you install full-height lengths of rebar, they may require bracing until the concrete hardens.

175

mortared stone walls 12

BUILDING A MORTARED STONE WALL requires more time and effort than constructing a dry-laid wall, but the mortared wall is sturdier and has a more formal, solid appearance. Mortared walls generally require less maintenance than dry-laid walls. Because the wall will have a foundation, check with your local building department to find out whether you need a building permit.

GENERAL REQUIREMENTS

Fitting the stones in a mortared wall is not as demanding as it is for a dry-laid wall—the mortar fills in gaps. For this reason, a mortared wall is a good option when you have a limited selection of stone shapes and sizes. It's the only option when you're working with river or creek stones—round creek-bed stones won't work in a dry-laid wall.

Mortar allows you to set irregularly shaped or rounded stones firmly, with the best faces exposed. Unlike dry-laid walls, which must slope inward as they go up, stone walls 3 feet and under are built with plumb sides. For a strong wall, however, it is good practice to use bond stones and to stagger the joints.

Mortar. The mortar mix used for stone walls is called a Type N mix. It consists of 1 part portland cement, 1 part lime, and 6 parts sand, all mixed with about 5 parts water. For small projects, it's usually best to buy premixed mortar in sacks; you just add the water. For larger projects, you can save money by buying the dry ingredients separately and making your own mortar mix. Some masons prefer to substitute fireclay for lime in the mix to make it more workable. Mixes containing lime can stain the stones, so if you use a lime mix, test it on your stones. Add water sparingly to make a dry, stiff mix that supports the stones and won't squeeze out of the joints.

The best way to compute the amount of mortar needed is to build a short section of mortared wall (3 x 5 feet, for example) and note the amount of mortar required. Multiply this amount by the number of 5-foot sections to figure out how much you'll need for the rest of the wall. Rubble and fieldstone walls will require more mortar than walls constructed of neatly fitting cut stones or ashlar.

FOOTINGS

MORTARED STONE WALLS are inflexible, and they require concrete footings as a result. For walls less than 2 feet high, the footing may be as simple as a shallow trench dug to the width of the wall and filled with several inches of concrete. For higher, wider walls, the footing should be twice the width of the wall. The footing should be as thick as the wall is wide. In cold climates, the footing should extend below the frost line. In some areas that would be 36 inches below the surface. Check with your building department to see what local code requires. The top of the footing should be several inches below ground level so that it won't show once you build the wall. (For complete instructions on installing wall footings, see Chapter 11, "Wall Foundations," page 164.) Allow the footing to cure for at least three days before building the wall.

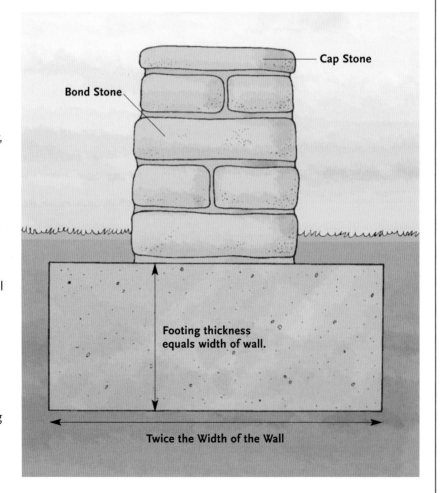

Cap Stone

Bond Stone

Footing thickness equals width of wall.

Twice the Width of the Wall

Height is a factor when you are considering whether to construct a mortared or a dry-laid wall. In this case, because the wall is over 4 feet, it requires the support offered by mortar.

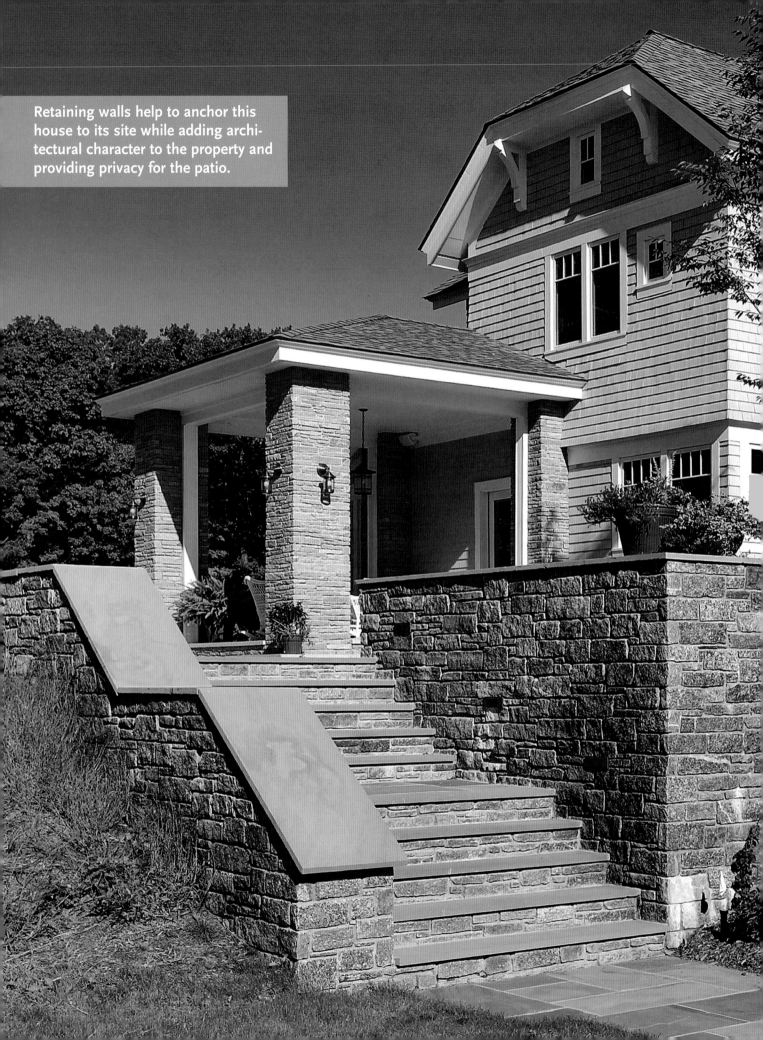

Retaining walls help to anchor this house to its site while adding architectural character to the property and providing privacy for the patio.

WALL CONSTRUCTION

Mortared stone walls are built much like dry-laid walls. The work will progress slower, but it requires less precise fitting of stones and therefore somewhat less skill. Select bond stones, end stones, and cap stones, and spread them along the course of the wall. Choose the remaining stones one course at a time, and test their fit without mortar first.

Place the end stones, and set bond stones every 4 to 6 feet along the foundation. Fit the remaining stones so that joints between them are narrow but no less than about ½ inch wide. Fill voids between large stones with smaller ones.

smart tip

USING A GROUT BAG

A GROUT BAG LOOKS MUCH THE SAME AS THE PASTRY BAGS CHEFS USE, BUT THIS HEAVY-DUTY VERSION SPEEDS UP GROUT APPLICATION AND REDUCES CLEAN UP TIME AS WELL. TO USE ONE, FILL IT WITH A SLIGHTLY SOUPY GROUT MIX; CLOSE THE END; AND SQUEEZE TO APPLY. THE BAG HELPS YOU GET GROUT INTO TIGHT SPOTS WITH A MINIMUM OF MESS.

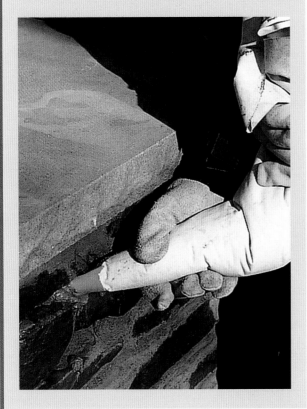

CONSTRUCTING A MORTARED STONE WALL

project

Once you're satisfied with the fit of the stones in your trial run, remove them, laying them in order to the side of the footing where you will use them. Make sure the stones are clean and dry before you set them permanently with mortar.

TOOLS & MATERIALS

- Work gloves ▪ Chalk-line box
- Stones ▪ Mortar
- Trowel ▪ Rubber mallet
- 2- or 4-ft. level ▪ Stakes
- Line level ▪ Jointing tool
- Whisk broom ▪ Cap stones
- Garden hose

3 Starting with the end stones, begin embedding all of the base stones in the mortar, following your dry-run arrangement. As you lay them in place, tap the stones lightly with a hammer or mallet until they are approximately level and even with one another. When you are satisfied with their position, use a pointed trowel to fill the gaps with mortar.

1 After the concrete footing cures for at least one week, gather all of your materials for the wall. Lay out your bond stones, end stones, and cap stones along the wall where they are close at hand but not in your way. Before bedding the first course of stones in mortar, do a dry run to test fit them in place. Use stones with flat surfaces for the first course.

2 Mix a batch of mortar that you can use within 30 minutes or so. Snap chalk lines on the footing to indicate the outer faces and ends of the wall; then use a mason's trowel to spread a 2-in.-thick layer of mortar about 3 ft. down the length of the wall. Work within your chalk lines to conserve mortar, which should be easily workable but not runny.

4 As you work upward, a level string line will help you to keep courses even and square across the face of the wall. When your first course is complete, set up stakes and a string line to gauge the straightness and alignment of the stones. Although the stones will vary in height, try to keep the courses level. Place a line level on the string to serve as a guide.

5 When the base course is aligned and level, begin the next row, and all succeeding courses, at a corner or wall end. These are your "lead" points, and positioning them correctly helps to ensure that the stones set between them will be level and square. Trowel a bed of mortar onto your first row, and settle each stone into it until level. Continued on next page.

Continued from previous page.

6 After building the leads, move your string line so that it is about 3 in. above the outside edge of the next course of stones. Fill in the areas between the leads with randomly shaped stones, using the string line and the leads as guides. Don't forget to install bond stones every 4 to 6 ft. to help tie the loose stones together and add strength to the wall.

7 Use a jointing tool or wood dowel to tool the joints as you complete each section of wall. Joints should be ½ to 1 in. deep. Deep joints are used with rough stone to emphasize shadow lines and for a more dramatic appearance, while shallow joints are recommended for dressed stones to show off the workmanship and clean, sharp lines of the cut.

10 Carefully lift the cap stones in place, and bed them in the mortar layer by tapping them lightly but firmly with a rubber mallet. Do not use a steel-face hammer or hand sledge for this—large cap stones are often expensive and difficult to obtain, and a sharp hammer blow on an unseen weak spot can crack or even break a thick stone slab.

11 After the mortar has had time to harden, brush off any bits of loose mortar, and clean the finished wall using a strong spray of water. Use a stiff bristle brush and a mild detergent to scrub off any mortar film remaining on the stone faces. For stubborn stains, wash down the wall with a strong cleaning solution, such as trisodium phosphate (TSP).

8 If you work carefully, there should be little loose mortar to clean up as you proceed. Use a stiff-bristle whisk broom to clean off mortar and smooth out the scraped joints as you work. Also, brush off any mortar from the face of the stones before it adheres. You may use a wire brush, but test it first; wire can leave scratch marks on soft stone.

9 To cap the wall, spread a thick layer of mortar over the top course of stone. You can cap a wall as soon as you complete it, or wait a day or two to give the mortar between the stones time to become firm and strong. A cap can consist of large, flat, natural slabs, or dressed stone. You can also simply use mortar, crowned slightly in the center, for the cap.

WEDGING-UP IRREGULAR STONES

SOME STONES HAVE SURFACES that are too irregular to seat properly on the course below. Temporarily prop them into a level position with one or two small wooden wedges. Wet the wedges (so they will be easier to remove later); insert them between these stones; and mortar the joint. When the mortar is firm, pull out the wedges and fill the holes with additional mortar.

concrete block walls 13

CONCRETE BLOCKS provide a relatively fast, inexpensive way to build sturdy masonry walls that don't require many tools or skills to construct. The large, uniformly sized blocks make the work go quickly. Unlike stone walls, which are typically built with double stacks of stones, a freestanding concrete-block wall can be built with a single stack of blocks. You may not be able to build the wall as quickly as an experienced mason, but you can work in stages at your convenience.

ABOUT CONCRETE BLOCK

Building concrete-block walls requires a lot of heavy lifting and hard work, so it's best to pace yourself according to your physical ability. Spend a few hours each evening after work, or spread the job over several weekends.

Unlike stone walls, which are usually built with two stacks of stones, or wythes, a freestanding concrete-block wall can be built with a single stack of blocks. A wall up to 3 feet tall usually requires no steel reinforcement, unless it serves as a retaining wall. (Higher walls require special techniques and are best left to professionals.)

Types of Block

Conventional concrete blocks are composed of portland cement, graded aggregate (crushed stone), and water. They weigh about 40 to 45 pounds each. The blocks are usually gray, although you can find them in several pastel or earth colors. Lighter-weight blocks, called cinder blocks, contain lightweight aggregate, such as expanded shale, clay, slate, or even pumice stone. Cinder blocks may be as light as 25 pounds. They are usually less expensive and easier with which to work, but they don't have the structural strength and impact resistance of heavier blocks. Cinder blocks aren't recommended for building retaining walls or any wall that could be hit accidentally by a car or snow thrower. For building 3-foot garden walls, however, cinder blocks will usually suffice. Local building codes may limit their use.

Most blocks for walls have two or three hollow cores (called "cells") to reduce their weight and to provide a place for rebar. The solid sections between the cells are called webs. On some blocks, the faces and webs are tapered to provide additional surface on the top of the block for mortar.

smart tip

PAINTING BLOCK WALLS

IF YOU WANT TO PAINT A BLOCK WALL, BE SURE TO WAIT UNTIL THE MORTAR HAS CURED COMPLETELY— ABOUT FIVE TO SEVEN DAYS. SCRUB ALL SURFACES WITH A SOLUTION OF TRISODIUM PHOSPHATE (TSP) AND WATER. RINSE THOROUGHLY, AND ALLOW TO DRY. CHOOSE PAINT RECOMMENDED FOR EXTERIOR MASONRY SURFACES. BECAUSE MASONRY WALLS ARE RELATIVELY ROUGH, USE A LONG-NAP ROLLER AND APPLY AT LEAST TWO COATS OF PAINT.

SHAPES AND SIZES

STANDARD CONCRETE BLOCKS have a nominal measurement of 8 x 8 x 16 inches. The actual size is 7⅝ x 7⅝ x15⅝ inches to allow for a ⅜-inch mortar joint. You should use the (larger) nominal dimensions when estimating the number of blocks required for the job. Blocks also come in nominal widths of 4, 6, 8, 10, and 12 inches. Narrower sizes are common in very low walls, planters, and garden borders.

Most wall construction involves two types of blocks—stretcher blocks and corner blocks. Stretcher blocks have two flanges at each end. Corner blocks have one flat end to provide a finished appearance at the end or corner of a wall. Half blocks are half the length of a standard block. You can also use them for building wall ends. Special solid-top blocks and cap blocks have smooth tops for finishing the top of the wall.

Specialty Blocks. Other specialty blocks are used for structural purposes in long or tall walls. Among these blocks are bond-beam blocks, pilaster (pier) blocks, and control-joint blocks. Bond-beam blocks have a U-shaped channel that you fill with mortar to strengthen the wall. Pilaster blocks are flat on both ends. Control-joint blocks have interlocking ends that are joined without mortar to allow for movement in the wall.

Decorative Blocks. You can also buy various types of decorative blocks, which have sculptured or patterned surfaces to add visual interest to the wall.

Screen blocks are narrow, lightweight blocks with patterned openings. The openings allow the passage of light and air through the wall while providing some privacy.

Because concrete blocks are manufactured locally, your choices will be limited to what's available at your local masonry supply or home center. Order decorative blocks or specialty blocks several weeks in advance.

TYPES OF BLOCK

Stretchers have end flanges that butt in a mortar joint.

End blocks have at least one finished end.

Cap blocks finish off the tops of block walls.

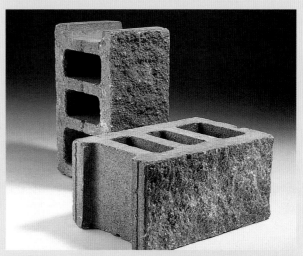

Rough-face blocks offer a textured, stonelike surface.

Interlocking blocks join without mortar.

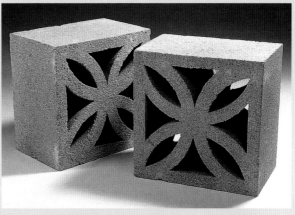

Decorative blocks have webs on the vertical faces.

189

Concrete-Block Walls

Basic Requirements

Concrete-block walls need a poured-concrete footing for support. In some cases, reinforcement also may be needed. You can reinforce a wall by filling the cores with mortar and steel rods (called "rebar") or by building a column (called a "pilaster"). Even low walls can fall apart if the cores aren't filled with concrete or if no rebar is used. Check local codes to see what's required in your area.

Footings and Foundations. Before you lay the first block, the footing must be poured, screeded, floated smooth, and allowed to cure fully. (See Chapter 11, "Wall Foundations," beginning on page 164.) Pour the footing to the thickness required by local building codes—typically 6 inches for 3-foot garden walls. To determine the required length of the footing, measure the length of the proposed wall, and add 4 to 6 inches at each end. Typically, a footing is twice as wide as the block you'll be using.

If the top of the footing will be below the frost line, you can build a foundation up to ground level using stretchers and end blocks. (See "Types of Block," page 188.) In some cases, the blocks below grade may need to be reinforced, usually by filling the block cavities with concrete or grout and inserting reinforcing rods. Check local codes for specific requirements in your area.

Mortar. Mortar for outdoor use is generally what is called Type N—1 part portland cement, 1 part hydrated lime, and 6 parts sand. For most residential wall projects, you're better off buying premixed mortar in sacks rather than mixing mortar from separate ingredients. Mortar mix should be somewhat drier than concrete. Test for the proper amount by creating a series of ridges in the mixture using a hoe or shovel. If the ridges remain sharp and distinct, you have added the right amount of water.

If you're constructing a below-grade concrete-block foundation, Type M mortar may be required. (Type N weathers better; Type M produces a stronger bond.) Type M consists of 1 part portland cement, ¼ part hydrated lime, and 3 parts sand. Check local codes to find out the type of mortar you should be using.

Control Joints. Control joints allow cracks to occur only at specific joints in the wall. On a small project, such as a short, low garden wall, you probably won't need control joints. However, long walls and those subject to unusual stresses will probably need control joints of some sort.

Because many variables determine how or where cracks may appear in a wall, there are no specific rules or guidelines on where control joints will be needed. Generally, cracks occur at changes in wall height or at changes in footing level, such as above a stepped footing on hillside walls. Cracks may also occur at changes in wall thickness—at a pilaster, for example. Long lengths of wall usually develop cracks due to uneven settling or movement of earth beneath the footing. As a rule of thumb, long walls should have control joints placed every 20 feet.

There are several ways you can incorporate control joints into a wall, but the easiest is to use special control-joint blocks. These are cast to form an interlocking tongue-and-groove joint. (The end of one block has a tongue; the other has a groove.) Lay half-size control-joint blocks every second course to create a straight control joint that runs from top to bottom of the wall. To allow for movement between the blocks, do not mortar the joint. Run a bead of flexible caulk into the control joint to hide the crack.

ESTIMATING AMOUNTS

BASE THE NUMBER OF BLOCKS you'll need on the block type's nominal dimensions, rather than on its actual dimensions. If possible, design the wall so that the height and length come out in multiples of the nominal dimensions of the blocks. For example, a standard block is nominally 8 x 8 x 16 inches, so a wall that's 8 inches wide, 32 inches high, and 8 feet long would require no cut blocks.

First, determine the length of the proposed wall in inches. Divide by the block length (typically 16 inches) to get the number of blocks needed for one course. Then divide the overall height of the wall by one block height (typically 8 inches) to determine the number of courses needed. Then multiply the blocks required along the length by the number of courses. Add 5 percent to allow for breakage. When figuring for walls with corners, measure the full length of each wall separately. A scale drawing of the wall will help you in your estimate. As a guide, plan on using about 113 standard-size blocks for every 100 square feet of wall.

PLANNING YOUR WALL

IF THE LENGTH OF YOUR WALL isn't an exact multiple of the block length plus mortar joints, you will have to cut the blocks. The most accurate way to cut concrete blocks is by using a masonry saw, which you can rent, or using a portable circular saw that is fitted with a masonry blade or an abrasive disc. If you have only a few blocks to cut, use a brick hammer and mason's chisel or brick set. Mark both sides of the block; then tap the chisel along the line.

■ **Bond Patterns.** Most standard blocks are laid in a simple running-bond pattern, in which the joints of each successive course are staggered by exactly half a block. This pattern provides the greatest strength for the wall. It also makes the best use of standard block sizes with a minimum amount of cut blocks. You can add interest to a bond pattern by combining concrete blocks of varying sizes. Other patterns include an off-set bond and a stacked bond. A stacked-bond pattern, with one joint directly above the next, is commonly used to construct screen-block walls. It isn't as structurally sound as the others, so it usually requires vertical reinforcement.

REINFORCING BLOCK WALLS

Vertical. Voids will align from top to bottom. Fill a void every 4 ft. with concrete (above left). Drive rebar into the still-wet concrete (above right). This provides top-to-bottom support.

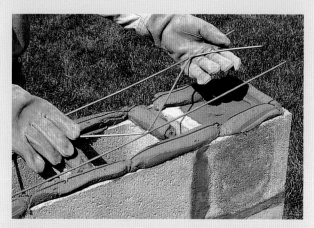

Horizontal. On every other course, spread an extra-thick layer of mortar (above left). Set block reinforcement wire into the mortar (above right). Sink the wire well into the mortar so it doesn't interfere with the bond.

A running-bond pattern, in which the joints are staggered by half a block, gives a wall the stability and strength its height requires.

BUILDING A BLOCK WALL

The following steps show how to lay the first course of a concrete-block wall. The instructions assume that you have already placed a suitable poured-concrete footing. You also should have the ingredients and tools for mixing mortar. As mentioned, concrete blocks do not need to be wet down before being laid.

Mark the Wall Ends or Corners. First, locate the outside corners or ends of the wall by stretching lines between the batter boards that you set up for the footing. On straight walls, hang a plumb bob at the wall's ends. If your wall has corners, hang it from the intersecting lines as well. Mark these spots on the footing with a pencil. With a helper, snap chalk lines on the footing to represent the outside edges of each wall.

smart tip

CUTTING CONCRETE BLOCK

YOU CAN PURCHASE HALF BLOCKS TO CREATE STAGGERED JOINTS IN THE COURSES, BUT SOMETIMES YOU WILL NEED TO TRIM A BLOCK. THE EASIEST WAY IS TO USE A CIRCULAR SAW WITH A MASONRY CUTTING BLADE. BE SURE TO WEAR EYE PROTECTION WHEN CUTTING ANY TYPE OF MASONRY.

project

BUILDING THE WALL

If possible, adjust the mortar joint spacing slightly so that you don't have to cut blocks. If you have to cut blocks, they must be at least one-half block long. Fill smaller spaces by cutting two blocks: for a space that is a one-quarter-block long, for example, cut two blocks to five-eighths their full length. Remove a block next to the gap. Fill the resulting gap with the cut blocks. Once all the blocks are laid out, check the corners to make sure that they meet at 90 degrees.

TOOLS & MATERIALS

- ▌Work gloves ▌Safety glasses ▌Plumb bob
- ▌Chalk-line box ▌Grease pencil ▌Concrete blocks
- ▌Wheelbarrow or mixer ▌Mortar ▌Level
- ▌Trowels and jointing tool ▌Mason's block and string
- ▌Control joints ▌Caulk ▌Bucket ▌Metal mesh
- ▌Rebar (optional) ▌Cap blocks (optional)

3 Butter the flanges, or ears, of the next block with mortar, and gently but quickly set it in place against the first block. Be careful not to push the first block out of position. Check the width of the joint between the blocks; then recheck that both blocks are level and aligned on your layout lines. If you are building a corner, check that it is square.

1 Before you begin mixing mortar and installing the blocks, do a dry run to check the alignment and spacing of the blocks to avoid awkward cuts. Use your layout lines, and hang a plumb bob to determine the exact placement of wall faces; then snap chalk lines and lay out the first course. Use a grease pencil to mark the position of key blocks.

2 Mix a stiff batch of mortar, and spread a 1-in.-thick bed for the starter blocks. Lay enough mortar to place several blocks, keeping the mortar within your layout lines. Position the first block, and align it with the layout lines. Tap the block lightly with the trowel handle to settle it into the mortar. Check that it is level and plumb in all directions.

4 After placing blocks at both ends of your wall, fill in the remaining "stretcher" blocks. Use mason's blocks and string, and adjust the mortar bed depth, if necessary, to keep this course straight and level. When you reach the last block to be installed in the row, called the "closure" block, butter both ends and carefully slide it into place to complete the first course.

5 With the first course completed, begin building up the leads, or corners, of the wall. Set as many blocks as needed in each corner to create a pyramid, culminating with one block at the top. To install each block, first trowel a 1-in.-thick strip of mortar onto just the top front edges of the blocks below it. Mortar all top edges to create a stronger wall. Continued on next page.

Concrete-Block Walls

Continued from previous page.

6 As you construct the leads, check frequently to make sure the blocks are plumb, level with one another, and in alignment from corner to corner. Much like stone wall construction, concrete block leads help to establish the integrity and appearance of the entire wall, so it is important that you take the time to build them correctly.

7 Another way to check the alignment of the leads is by holding a straightedge across the corners of the blocks as the rows stack up. Although a long level is shown here, any type of straightedge can be used. This test ensures that vertical joints are equally spaced. In full-block corners, all joints should be centered on the blocks below and above.

10 Remove excess material using a trowel. After the mortar starts to set up, use a jointing tool to shape and finish the vertical and horizontal joints (inset). Flush joints that are even with the blocks faces are preferred for walls to be covered with stucco. If the joints will remain exposed, create shallow concave joints to shed water; but be careful not to rake too deep.

11 To cap a concrete-block wall, you can fill the voids of the top course of blocks with mortar. To do this, first lay a strip of metal mesh atop the next-to-last course. This prevents the mortar from falling through into the cavities below. The mesh should be available from your concrete supplier in sizes to match the width of your block wall.

8 After the leads are built up at wall ends or corners, install line blocks for the next course of stretcher blocks to be added, and connect the mason's blocks with builder's string. Use a line level, and position the string even with the tops of the blocks. Align each course to the string, adding or removing mortar between the rows to keep them level.

9 Control joints at varying intervals in a row of blocks help to relieve stresses in long walls to prevent joint cracks. Use special control-joint concrete blocks, which have material at the ends that will not bond to mortar, or install felt paper between blocks as you work. When you've completed the row or the entire wall, fill these joints with flexible caulk.

12 Spread a continuous layer of mortar over the mesh; then lay the top course of blocks as you normally would. Fill all of the voids in this top course with mortar. You can insert chunks of broken block and small stones into the mortar to help fill the spaces and conserve material. Strike off the mortar so that it is even with the surface of the blocks.

13 For a finished appearance, set solid concrete cap blocks in mortar along the top of the wall. Be sure to order cap blocks sized to the same width as your wall blocks. You can also set small stones in a bed or mortar (inset). Square-cut natural stone is another alternative, or you can build up the mortar to form its own raised-crown cap.

FINISHING IN STUCCO

Bare concrete-block walls aren't very attractive, no matter how you've designed and built them. At the very least, you'll probably want to give them a coat of paint. Other treatments for masonry walls include stucco and brick or stone veneers.

Stucco is a popular surfacing material. Many textures and effects are possible; rough textures tend to hide minor imperfections on wall surfaces. (See "Stucco Finishes," page 200.) Usually, stucco is applied in its natural gray color and painted later, but color powder may be mixed into the material before application. If applied properly, stucco is durable and can be used in many climates. However, stucco work takes skill, and once you start applying a coat, you must finish the entire surface.

APPLYING STUCCO

IF YOU ARE PLANNING TO STUCCO a concrete-block wall, strike the mortar joints flush as you build. Then you can apply stucco directly to the wall in either two or three coats. Either way, the first coat is the scratch coat; it literally gets scratched to receive the second coat. The second coat is called the brown coat. It is mixed and applied the same way as the scratch coat. The optional third coat is the finish coat. It's a thinner coat made of white cement and white stucco sand for a white appearance. Or, you can add color pigment to the mix. The pigment is available in a variety of earth tones. The wall should be clean and damp (but not wet) before applying stucco. The project shown is a two-coat stucco wall.

smart tip

MAKE A RAKING TOOL

Cut a length of 1x2, and hammer in galvanized roofing nails every ¾ in.

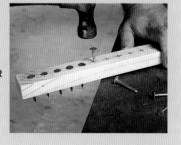

APPLYING STUCCO TO CONCRETE-BLOCK WALLS

project

Clean the wall. Then install base strip bead to keep the stucco off the ground. Attach a corner bead where necessary. Make up a mix of 1 part mortar cement and 4 parts sand, and add just enough water to make the mix workable. Starting at the bottom of the wall and using a flat, square trowel, apply a ¼-inch-thick coat of stucco over the surface.

TOOLS & MATERIALS

- Work gloves
- Base and corner bead
- Masonry nails ▪ Stucco mix
- Mixing tray ▪ Trowels
- Raking tool ▪ Spray bottle
- Level ▪ Finishing float
- Plastic sheeting

3 If you want a durable, three-layer coat of stucco, apply the second layer (called a "brown" coat) as soon as possible after the scratch coat sets up but before this layer hardens completely. If you wait until the scratch coat hardens, apply a light spray of water to the surface before applying the finish coat. This will help this final layer to adhere.

1 Bare concrete-block walls often require a decorative surface treatment, such as stucco, which is easy to apply and can be finished in a variety of ways. Begin by attaching a metal base strip and corner beads where appropriate. Use galvanized nails or self-tapping deck screws to fasten the metal strips. Apply a ¼ in. coat of stucco with a flat trowel.

2 The first coat of stucco is called a "scratch" coat. While the stucco is still wet, use a suitable tool to scratch or rake the surface in order to provide a purchase, or "tooth," for the following coat. Be careful not to rake too deep or peel the stucco layer from the wall—you just want to roughen the surface, so scratch about half the depth of the top layer.

4 Allow the first two layers to cure for a few days before applying the finish layer of stucco, which is variously called a "white" coat or topcoat. If desired, you can mix a powder coloring agent into the stucco for this layer when you prepare it. Apply a ¼-in.-thick coat using a flat steel trowel. You can also tool a finish pattern into this surface while it is still workable.

5 Use plastic sheeting to cover the completed stucco for at least 48 hrs. This will retard drying time and keep the stucco moist as it cures. Do not press the plastic against the stucco. If the wall surface is in full sun or the weather is very warm and dry, apply an occasional light mist of water to prevent the mortar from drying too quickly and cracking.

STUCCO FINISHES

Floated Smooth

Sponge Swirled

Brush Lined

Brush Splattered

Flattened Splatter

Board Dragged

Trowel Swirled

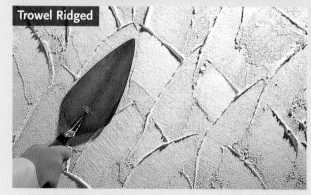
Trowel Ridged

A concrete-block wall can be as elegant as the way you chose to finish it. The material, finished simply, looks perfectly compatible within this somewhat formal setting.

brick walls

14

BRICK IS AN ATTRACTIVE WALL-BUILDING MATERIAL that is available in a variety of sizes, colors, and surface textures. You can set it in many different bond patterns and finish the joints in a number of different profiles. A typical wall is either one brick thick, known as "single wythe," or two bricks thick, known as "double wythe." Usually, brick walls under 2 feet high require no steel reinforcement. Taller walls may incorporate steel ties or even metal reinforcement into the design to withstand stresses and loads placed on the wall.

Brick Walls

BRICK BASICS

Many different types of brick are available, but those used for walls fall into three broad categories: building brick, face brick, and concrete brick. Within each of these categories, you'll find a wide variety of sizes, shapes, colors, and surface textures.

Building Brick. Also called common brick, building bricks are economical and are suitable for building low, informal garden walls. They may be a bit too rustic where a neat, formal look is desired. Building bricks are usually the "seconds" or "rejects" from the brickyard. Some bricks may be chipped, warped, or broken. Also, color, dimensions, and density may vary from brick to brick.

Face Brick. If a neat appearance is important, use face bricks. Compared with building brick, face brick is uniform in size, color, and surface texture. Face bricks come in a great variety of colors and textures and are the standard brick used in most outdoor construction. They're more expensive than building bricks, but because they're more uniform in size and shape, they're easier to work with than building brick. They also have a better finished appearance and are suitable for formal projects.

Concrete Brick. As the name implies, these bricks are formed from concrete. They cost considerably less than either type of clay brick. Concrete bricks are similar in appearance to concrete blocks, with a slightly rougher, more porous surface than clay bricks. Colors usually are limited to light or medium brick red or adobe beige. Concrete bricks don't have the strength of clay bricks, so they are prone to cracking, especially under severe freeze-thaw conditions. Check with your local building department to see whether these bricks are recommended for your particular project. If you use concrete bricks, plan to seal them with a waterproof masonry sealer. Ask the dealer for the appropriate product.

BRICK SIZES

MOST BRICKS come in modular sizes. The length of the most common modular unit, a standard brick, is roughly twice its width and three times its thickness. The nominal dimensions are 2⅔ x 4 x 8 inches. The actual brick is smaller than this by the thickness of a mortar joint—either ⅜ inch or ½ inch. Size varies for another reason, too: manufacturing tolerances. In any given production run, brick sizes can vary as much as ½ inch. If you're concerned about size, ask the dealer for the dimensions of the brick you intend to use. Other types of bricks used in wall construction include jumbo, Roman, Norman, SCR, and utility.

Some bricks used for walls have hollow cores to reduce their weight, provide a better mortar bond, and allow space to insert vertical reinforcing rods when constructing a tall wall, when required. While hollow-core bricks are sometimes less expensive than solid ones, you generally have fewer choices in size, color, and surface texture.

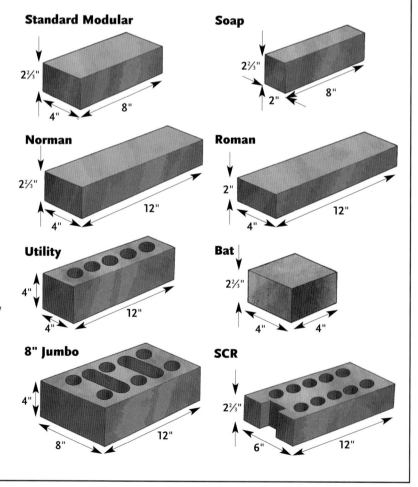

TYPES OF BRICK WALLS

Besides the look of the bricks themselves, two factors determine a brick wall's appearance. One is the number of wythes used to build up the wall thickness; the other is the bond pattern in which you lay the bricks.

Wythes. A wall that is only one brick wide (4 inches wide if you're using standard bricks) is a single-wythe wall. Adding a second, parallel course of bricks next to the first one creates a double-wythe wall. A double-wythe wall is stronger than a single wythe, and the thicker wall may look more appropriate with other landscape features. Depending on the desired overall width of the wall, you may butt the wythes together (with a mortar joint between them) to produce a wall that is 8 inches wide, or you can space them apart to provide additional width. In the latter case, the cavity between the two wythes may be filled with grout (thinned mortar) or concrete (and sometimes reinforcing rods) to provide additional strength for tall walls. In all cases, the two wythes are tied together, either by bricks (called "headers"), metal masonry ties, or a combination of these, depending on the bond pattern. (For more on tying wythes together, see "Reinforcement," page 208.)

The slim, curved line created by this single-wythe brick wall adds an interesting feature to the landscape.

Brick Walls

Bond Patterns. The drawing opposite shows the popular running-bond pattern for brick walls. Some patterns—such as the common bond, Flemish bond, and English bond—are structural bonds. They incorporate header bricks to tie the wythes together. Running bond and stack bond usually require metal masonry ties to reinforce the wall. Single-wythe walls typically use a running-bond, offset running-bond, or stack-bond pattern. In the first two, the vertical joints are offset to provide additional strength. In a stack bond (also called Jack-on-Jack), the bricks are simply stacked one atop the other so that all vertical joints are aligned. A stack bond has virtually no lateral strength, depending almost entirely on the strength of the mortar joints to hold it together. Such walls are typically reinforced with masonry ties in horizontal joints. If vertical reinforcement is needed, use hollow-core bricks and insert rebar into the cores, as required by code. Check with your local building department for specific requirements.

A tall brick wall and archway that has been properly reinforced will stand the test of time.

WORKING WITH BRICK

Building a sturdy brick wall depends on three factors: a strong footing, adequate reinforcement, and proper mortar mix to bond the bricks together. Lacking any one of these elements, the wall will soon crack and eventually fall apart.

Footings

As a rule, a poured-concrete footing should be two times wider than the wall it supports and as thick as the wall is wide. The footing should also extend 4 to 6 inches beyond the ends of the wall. In severe winter climates, the footing must be below the frost line, which may be 36 inches or more. You can build the foundation up to ground level with concrete blocks. Usually, the top of the footing or foundation will be a few inches below grade, where it won't be seen. Fill the foundation-block cavities with mortar, and insert reinforcing rods.

Be sure to check local codes for specific footing and foundation requirements. (Complete instructions for constructing footings appear in Chapter 11, on page 168.)

ESTIMATING AMOUNTS

BRICKS ARE MORE EXPENSIVE than most other masonry products. You buy bricks by the piece. You may get a discount if you buy a whole pallet. As with lumber, you can sometimes go into the yard and hand-pick bricks out of the pile.

The number of bricks you'll need depends on the size of the wall, the number of wythes, the size of the bricks, mortar-joint spacing, and the bond pattern. Bond patterns that include header bricks will require more than those that use only stretchers.

A simple way to calculate is to make a scale elevation drawing for a 2- to 4-foot section of the wall you're building. In your drawing, include the bond pattern and the overall height of the wall. Draw in the bricks at their nominal, rather than actual size, and you'll be able to leave the mortar joints out of your drawing. Count the bricks in the section, and multiply the number of bricks required for each section by the number of sections required to complete the wall. Add 5 to 10 percent extra to allow for miscuts, breakage, and future repairs.

ANATOMY OF A BRICK WALL

AS IN OTHER TRADES, brick masons have terms to describe the components of their handiwork. Learning these terms will help you understand the instructions in this chapter. One horizontal row of bricks is called a "course." Masons identify each one as odd (first, third, fifth) and even (second, fourth, sixth) courses, starting from the base of the wall up. When building the wall, you'll get the best results by building the ends of the wall (the "leads") first, rather than laying complete courses from one end of the wall to the other. Leads help to establish proper alignment of vertical mortar joints and let you attach a mason's line at each end to keep the wall straight and level. The last brick you lay in each course is called the "closure brick." Even if you take considerable care in laying out the wall, the closure bricks often must be cut to fit.

Stretchers and Headers. Stretchers are bricks laid flat with the long dimension parallel with the length of the wall. If the brick is laid on edge, it's called a "rowlock stretcher." Bricks laid flat at right angles to the stretchers, tying the two wythes together, are "headers." A header laid on edge becomes a "rowlock header." Header courses may be used to cap the wall.

Bats and Soaps. "Bats" are bricks cut in half across their width. Bricks cut along their length are called "soaps." Both are sometimes available precut, but more likely, you'll need to cut them yourself. Bats are commonly used in single-wythe walls to finish the ends and to produce various patterns.

Head Joints and Bed Joints. Vertical mortar joints between bricks are called "head joints"; horizontal joints between courses are called "bed joints."

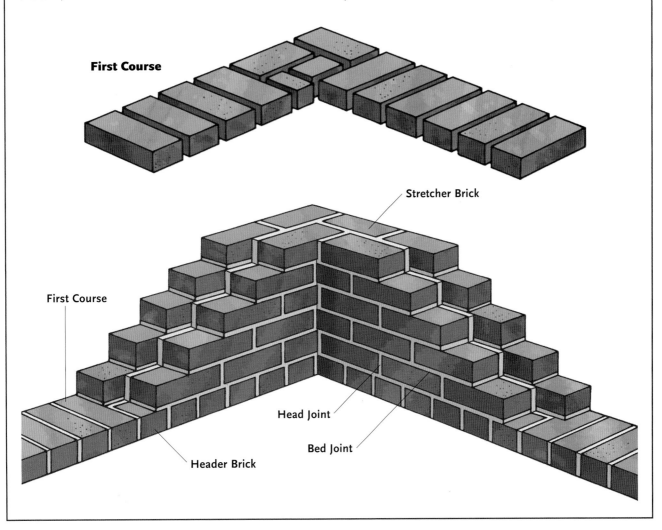

First Course

Stretcher Brick

First Course

Head Joint

Bed Joint

Header Brick

Brick Walls

Reinforcement

Requirements for wall reinforcement will vary depending on wall height, bond pattern, soil stability, wind load, and other factors. Check with your building department for accepted practices and code requirements. For most walls up to 3 feet high, a structural bond pattern, such as common bond, provides sufficient strength without reinforcement. Double-wythe walls that are set in a stacked-bond or running-bond pattern are usually tied together with metal Z-ties embedded in the mortar; tall walls may also require reinforcement with metal rebar. (See "Wall Reinforcement," at right.)

Z-Ties. Steel Z-ties are used to tie wythes together in a double-wythe wall. Typically, the ties are placed in a bed joint spaced 36 inches apart (or as required by code) along every third or fourth course. Stagger the ties so that they do not align vertically.

Reinforcement Bar. Steel bars, known as "rebar," come in many different diameters and are designated by numbers, such as #3 or #4, for example. The numbers correspond to ⅛-inch increments—#3 rebar is ⅜ inch in diameter, #4 is ½ inch in diameter, and so on. Rebar is inserted into the concrete footing; it extends up between wythes in a double-wythe wall or through brick cores in a single-wythe wall. You can cut rebar with a hacksaw.

Pilasters. Pilasters, or built-in columns, are sometimes incorporated into brick walls to provide additional strength. Typically, the pilasters are located at both ends or corners and at 10- to 12-foot intervals along the length of the wall. The use of pilasters is especially recommended for single-wythe walls.

Pilasters are tied into the wall with header bricks and Z-ties. In double-wythe walls, the cavity in the pilaster is filled with grout (mortar that has been thinned so it can be poured) or concrete and reinforced with rebar. In all cases, the poured-concrete footing should follow the shape of the pilasters. Consult your building department to see whether pilasters are required for your wall design and the type that is recommended. Even if they aren't required, pilasters can lend visual interest to a wall. Several basic designs are shown in "Pilaster Reinforcement," bottom.

WALL REINFORCEMENT

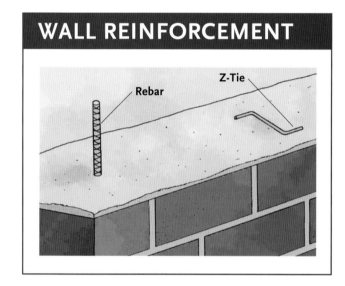

Rebar

Z-Tie

PILASTER REINFORCEMENT

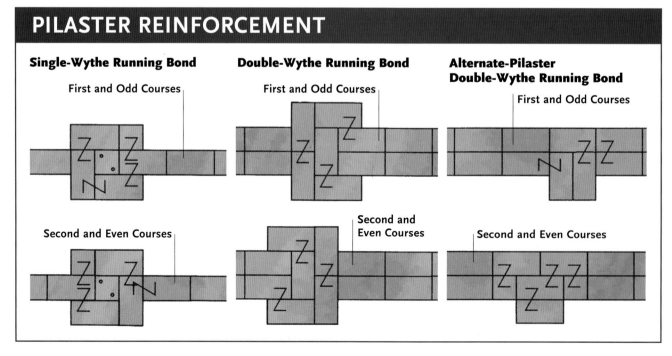

Single-Wythe Running Bond

First and Odd Courses

Second and Even Courses

Double-Wythe Running Bond

First and Odd Courses

Second and Even Courses

Alternate-Pilaster Double-Wythe Running Bond

First and Odd Courses

Second and Even Courses

A tall brick privacy wall captures the mood of an English garden, especially when it is accented by lush plantings. White lattice enhances the look and a concrete-ball finial on the top at the corner adds a classical note.

MORTAR

MORTAR IS A MIXTURE OF CEMENT, hydrated lime, sand, and water. Type N mortar is most often used for freestanding brick garden walls. However, you should consult a local masonry dealer for the best type to use for your project. As a rule, increasing the proportions of lime and sand in relationship to cement makes mortar less expensive and more workable, but weaker. The table below shows mortar mixtures and their applications.

For most residential walls, it's more convenient to buy premixed mortar in bags than to mix the components yourself. A 70-pound bag of premixed mortar is enough to set about 40 standard bricks.

Mortar Consistency. As with bagged dry-mix concrete, you'll need to add the correct amount of water to achieve the desired consistency. This may take some experimentation. Generally, stiffer mixes are used for concrete block, while wetter mixes are used for bricks. You can mix mortar with a shovel or hoe in a wheelbarrow, in a concrete barge, or on a large sheet of plywood. A power mixer is recommended for large jobs to speed the mixing and to save your back. Work in small batches at first. If the mortar starts to get dry, you can add a bit more water to bring it back to the proper consistency. This process, called "retempering the mortar," can be done only one time for each batch. Additional retempering severely weakens the mix.

Grout. Grout is thin, pourable mortar. It's made by adding enough water to the mortar mix to make it soupy. You can use grout, and sometimes vertical rebar, to fill the cavity between a double-wythe wall. Pour the grout as you work—after laying several courses of a wall, pour grout into the cavity with a coffee can. Then lay a few more courses. Repeat the process to the full height of the wall. Whether or not you need to add grout or other reinforcement depends on soil conditions and the wall's function and design. Check with your building department.

For a neat look, clean off mortar that drips onto the face of the brick before it dries.

TYPES OF MORTAR

Type	Proportions of Ingredients	Recommended for:
M	1 Cement ¼ Hydrated lime 3 Sand	Foundations, walks, retaining walls, and wherever masonry will have a long-term contact with damp earth
S	1 Cement ¼-½ Hydrated lime 4½ Sand	Reinforced masonry and wherever high-bond strength is needed, such as walls in windy areas
N	1 Cement ¼-½ Hydrated lime 6 Sand	Weather-exposed structures, such as above-grade garden walls

TOOLING MORTAR JOINTS

■ **Extruded joints.** Extruded joints require no tooling; they are formed naturally as mortar squeezes out between the bricks when you tap them in place. Such joints are used where a rustic appearance or texture is desired, but they tend to trap water, making them relatively weak. Also, pieces of mortar often break away, leaving an unattractive finish. Using a masonry sealer will help extend the life of these joints. (Ask your masonry dealer for the appropriate product.)

■ **Flush joints.** To create a flush joint, simply cut away the excess mortar with the edge of your trowel as you lay the bricks. Flush joints produce a smooth surface and are often used for brick walls that will be painted or stuccoed. Left unpainted, the joints are not particularly watertight, and surface layers may eventually flake off or crack.

■ **Concave joints.** These joints are the most popular because they shed water well. To make these joints, press a convex jointer into the mortar and slide it along the joint. The tool compresses the mortar, making a strong, watertight joint. Walls with concave joints have a flat look, with little or no shadow.

■ **V-joints.** These joints are made by removing mortar with a pointed tool called a "V-jointer." V-joints emphasize shadows and allow good water runoff, making them relatively watertight joints.

■ **Raked joints.** These joints are recessed about ½ inch back from the face of the wall, using a tool called a "rake-out jointer." Raked joints create dark shadows for a dramatic effect. However, they collect water and may promote moss growth.

■ **Weathered joints and struck joints.** Make these by removing mortar with the point of a mason's trowel. Orient the trowel tip upward for weathered joints, downward for struck joints. Both joints produce attractive shadow lines. For practical purposes, weathered joints shed water better than struck joints.

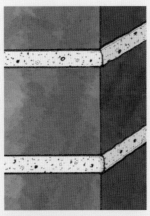
Extruded Joint

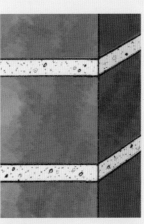
Flush Joint

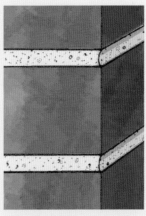
Concave Joint

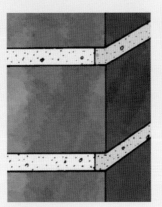
V-Joint

Raked Joint

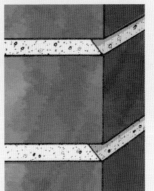
Weathered Joint

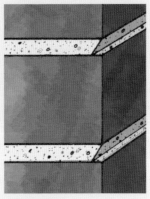
Struck Joint

A single-wythe brick wall serves as a planter box for this multilevel outdoor living space. The traditional look of brick suits the home's architecture.

BUILDING A SINGLE-WYTHE WALL

project

The following steps show how to lay a single-wythe brick wall in a running-bond pattern. The instructions assume that you have already poured a suitable footing and will be providing any reinforcement required by local building codes. First, thoroughly spray all the bricks in with a garden hose an hour or two before laying them. By the time you get the mortar mixed, the surface water should have evaporated from the bricks, leaving them slightly damp. Do not lay bricks that are dripping wet.

TOOLS & MATERIALS

▌Concrete footing ▌Work gloves ▌Brick
▌Spacers ▌Pencil ▌Chalk-line box
▌Mortar ▌Trowel ▌Z-ties ▌Spirit Level
▌Story pole ▌Mason's line and blocks
▌Striking tool

1 Before you mix the mortar and begin building the wall, do a trial run with the first course to work out any spacing and alignment problems. Place the bricks without mortar, using wood spacers, and adjust the joint gaps as needed to fit your intended layout. When you are satisfied with the spacing, use a pencil to mark the position of the mortar joints.

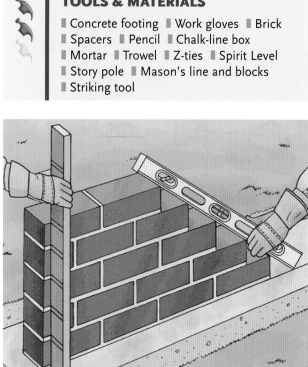

4 Working from the end, build the leads three to five courses high before you fill in the center sections. If Z-ties are required, insert them in the horizontal joints. Check course heights using a story pole, which you can make from a straight 1x4. A brick can be your guide for the lines. Check for plumb and level often. The level should touch each brick, as shown.

5 Attach line blocks to the second course of bricks in each lead. If the string sags, support it with a brick. Use wood spacers to simulate mortar. A fold of flashing can hold the string in place. The last or "closure" brick in each course must fit neatly between the two bricks on either side. Measure very carefully, and you may not need cut bricks or fractional size bricks, called "bats."

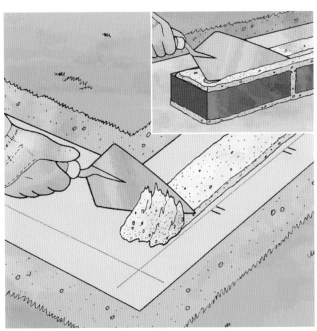

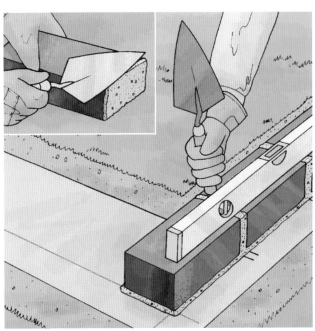

2 Measure and snap chalk lines on the footings to mark the front face of the wall. Lay a continuous 1-in.-thick bed of mortar along the line, but be careful not to obscure the chalk line or your joint spacing marks. When you lay mortar for succeeeding courses, apply the mortar to the top edges of the bricks (inset). Make the mortar edges thicker than the center for top courses.

3 Butter the brick edges with mortar (inset); then lay the bricks in place. Check with a level. Tap a too-high brick with the trowel handle. Add mortar under a low brick. Next, attach a string to line blocks at each end that is even with the tops of the bricks. If they are a bit out of level, trowel mortar under the low end or lay thicker bed joints at the low ends over a few courses.

6 As you get ready to lay each course, reset your line blocks at both ends of the row and check the string with a line level. Pull the string taut, and align it with the top outer edge of the bricks in the row. For the best appearance, stagger the closure bricks so that they do not align vertically. Clean any mortar from the brick faces as you work.

smart tip

FINISHING THE MORTAR JOINTS

USE YOUR TROWEL TO SMOOTH ANY SQUEEZED-OUT MORTAR FLUSH ALONG THE JOINTS. KEEP YOUR EYE ON THE JOINTS AS YOU WORK, AND TEST THEM BY PRESSING YOUR THUMB GENTLY INTO THE MORTAR. IF YOUR THUMBPRINT REMAINS AND THE MORTAR DOESN'T STICK TO YOUR HAND, THEN IT'S TIME TO TOOL THE MORTAR JOINTS. SELECT THE APPROPRIATE TOOL FOR THE TYPE OF JOINT YOU WANT TO MAKE. (SEE "TOOLING MORTAR JOINTS," ON PAGE 211.) TOOL THE VERTICAL JOINTS FIRST, AND THEN WORK ON THE HORIZONTAL JOINTS. FINISH BY BRUSHING THE JOINTS LIGHTLY WITH A WHISK BROOM OR SOFT-BRISTLE BRUSH.

BUILDING A DOUBLE-WYTHE WALL

For a double-wythe wall, lay each course two bricks wide, tying the wythes together with header bricks, masonry ties, or a combination of these. Mark the footing to locate the outside and inside edges. For straight walls with no corners, lay a dry course. Space the wythes so that the cap bricks will overhang each side of the wall by about ¼ inch. Mark the brick locations; remove them; and lay a mortar bed that is long enough for three bricks and narrower than the wall by ½ inch on each side.

TOOLS & MATERIALS

▌ Concrete footing ▌ Work gloves ▌ Brick
▌ Spacers ▌ Pencil ▌ Chalk-line box ▌ Mortar
▌ Trowel ▌ Mason's line and blocks
▌ Spirit Level ▌ Framing square ▌ Z-ties
▌ Story pole ▌ Striking tool ▌ Metal flashing

1 Start with a dry-run layout to check joint and unit spacing. When ready, spread mortar and place three bricks in each wythe; then recheck their alignment. Repeat this procedure at the other end of the wall. Run a mason's line from the end bricks to check whether they are level with each other. Build up the mortar bed under one end if necessary; then fill in the rest of the course.

You can cap a brick wall with brick or a number of other materials, such as concrete or natural stone with a chiseled or bullnose edge. Here, capping the wall with brick lends uniformity to the wall's design.

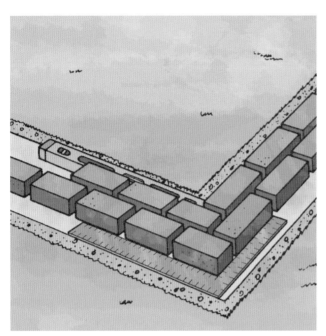

2 If the wall turns 90 deg., use a framing square to make sure the corner is square. Or for greater accuracy over long runs, use the "3-4-5" measurement system: first, measure and mark 3 ft. from the corner in one direction; then measure 4 ft. from the corner in the other direction. If the distance between these two points is exactly 5 ft., the corner is square.

3 After laying the first course, build up the ends, or leads, to 5 bricks in height. As you build up the leads, lay metal reinforcing ties in the mortar to tie the wythes together. The ties should be about 1 in. shorter than the wall width. Check constantly for plumb, level, and square. Use a story pole to ensure consistent wall heights. (See step 4 on page 214.)

4 Place bricks in each wythe as you work down the length of the wall. Attach line blocks and string at the top of the lowest course. Depending on the design, some walls are solid from front to back, with mortar or grout filling the joint between the double brick rows. Complete each course with a closure brick. When the mortar will hold a thumbprint, tool the joints.

5 A cap is optional if the wall is solid and the center joint is mortared closed. Among other things, you can place header bricks flat across the width of the wall. For a stronger cap, use rowlock headers laid on edge, as shown. If the cap overhangs the wall, adjust the joint space or score and cut a unit to fit. Place metal flashing in the bed joint for additional moisture protection.

retaining walls 15

RETAINING WALLS prevent soil at a higher grade level from tumbling down or eroding to a lower grade. Retaining walls can transform a slope into a series of terraces for lawns, planting beds, or patio areas. On flat sites, low retaining walls can create raised planting beds or borders, adding a sense of visual depth to the landscape.

RETAINING-WALL BASICS

You can make retaining walls from a variety of materials: timber, stone, brick, and concrete block among them. Perhaps the easiest materials for the do-it-yourselfer to work with are mortarless interlocking concrete blocks designed especially for retaining walls. These blocks are discussed in "Interlocking Concrete-Block Walls," page 226. Timber retaining walls are also easy to build.

No matter which material you choose, retaining walls must be strong enough to hold the weight of the soil placed against them. And you must make provisions for drainage. With tall retaining walls, structural and drainage issues become critical, so it's best to leave the design and construction of tall walls to professionals. Retaining walls smaller than 3 feet high may be designed and built by the do-it-yourselfer, but check with the local building department.

Excavation

The type of excavation required to install the wall depends on wall height, the angle of the slope, and the amount of flat space you wish to create on the downhill side of the wall. On sloped ground, you'll generally cut and fill to create a flat area bounded by a low retaining wall. In the cut-and-fill process, you remove the soil downhill from the proposed wall.

If you're building a single retaining wall, it's easiest to cart the soil downhill and fill in the slope with it. Fill the excavated area behind the wall with tamped sand or gravel to facilitate drainage, and top it off with a layer of topsoil. If you're building a series of terraces and walls, it's easiest to dump the soil into a pile uphill. Fill the area immediately behind the wall as described as before. Then level off the slope from the pile.

Equipment. You can excavate low, short walls with a shovel, pick, and wheelbarrow. Heavy equipment, such as bulldozers, backhoes, and front-end loaders, may be required for larger projects. Unless you know how to operate such equipment, leave the job to an excavation contractor. Even for low walls, you'll need to move a lot of soil, so consider hiring a few strong backs to help with the shovel work.

DRAINAGE SYSTEMS

YOU'LL NEED A DRAINAGE SYSTEM for a retaining wall. Backfill the wall with gravel; lay perforated pipe; and build weep holes into the wall. The gravel drains water away from the wall, and the drainpipe carries water away from the wall footing. Line the excavation with permeable landscape fabric to keep silt from clogging the gravel—and make sure you're not directing the water runoff into a neighbor's yard.

For brick and block walls, you can make weep holes by omitting the mortar from some of the vertical (head) joints near the wall base. Or you can insert 1- or 2-inch-diameter PVC pipes in the head joints every 4 to 6 feet along the base of the wall as you build it. (See "Building a Block Wall," on page 194.) If you are building a timber wall, the pipes can be inserted in holes drilled in the wood. In all cases, cover the back of the hole with landscape fabric or fine galvanized wire mesh to help prevent clogging.

Dry-laid retaining walls of stone or interlocking blocks usually require no weep holes because there's no mortar between joints to block drainage.

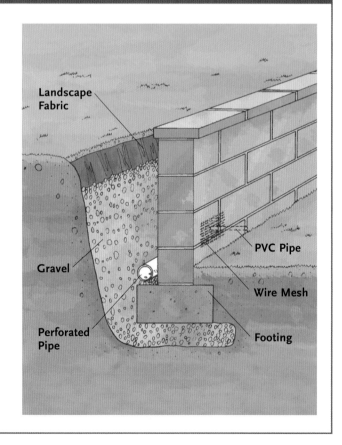

Landscape Fabric

Gravel

Perforated Pipe

PVC Pipe

Wire Mesh

Footing

Footings and Reinforcement

Most retaining walls require large, sturdy footings for support. (See Chapter 11, "Wall Foundations," beginning on page 164.) Specific requirements depend on soil conditions, the size and type of wall, and building codes. The width of the footing should be at least two-thirds the total wall height. The top of the footing should be at least 12 inches below grade on the downhill side of the wall. The footing should be as thick as the wall width or a minimum of 8 inches. All dimensions may vary, depending on local building codes.

Mortared masonry retaining walls usually have poured-concrete footings with steel reinforcement bar (rebar) running the length of the footing. Separate rebar extends vertically up into the wall to tie it to the footing. Typically, more of the footing extends behind the wall (uphill side) than in front of it, allowing the weight of the soil to keep the wall and footing from tilting forward. The exact orientation of the wall on the footing depends on code and specific site requirements.

Dry-laid stone retaining walls generally don't require poured-concrete footings or reinforcement. Large stones at the base of the wall serve as footings, and planting the crevices between the stones with ground covers or vines helps stabilize the wall and prevents soil erosion.

Pressure-treated landscape timbers will require some heavy lifting to install but only basic carpentry skills.

Stacked interlocking concrete blocks offer another relatively easy solution to building a low retaining wall without mortar.

In addition to its practical function, a retaining wall can add beauty to a home landscape. This stone wall provides a sturdy, handsome foundation for a hillside bed of flowers and shrubs.

LANDSCAPE-TIMBER WALLS

This wall is made of stacked landscape timbers tied together with lengths of ¾-inch rebar. To help resist the pressure of the soil against the wall, install timbers that reach into the hillside (called "deadmen"). They should be at least 3 feet long and cut from the same size timber as the rest of the wall. Walls between 3 and 4 feet need additional reinforcement and may require a concrete footing.

TOOLS & MATERIALS

▌Work gloves and safety glasses ▌Stakes
▌String ▌Shovels ▌Wheelbarrow
▌Gravel ▌Tamper ▌Circular saw
▌Treated landscape timbers
▌Landscape fabric ▌¾-in. drill ▌#6 Rebar
▌Perforated drainage pipes ▌¾-in. auger bit
▌Sledgehammer ▌12-in. galvanized spikes

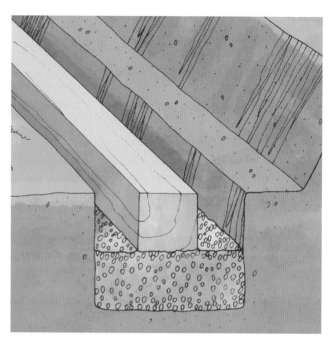

1 Excavate the wall location, and dig out an additional foot or two behind it to allow room to work. Set stakes, and use a string line to mark the wall; then dig a trench twice the depth of the first timber. Place 6 in. of gravel in the trench for drainage and to prevent frost heave. Lay the first timber course on top of the gravel, and level it into position.

LANDSCAPE-TIE WALL

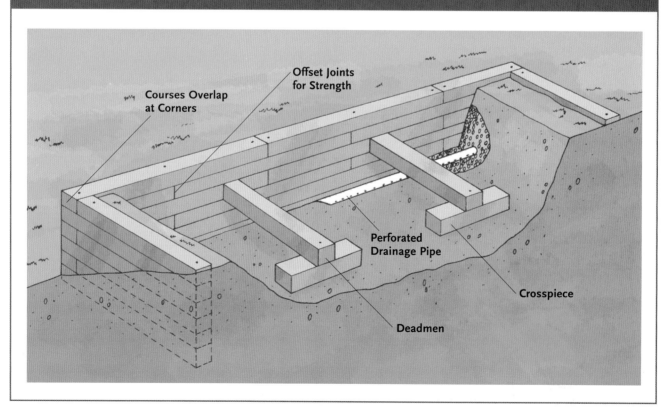

Courses Overlap at Corners

Offset Joints for Strength

Perforated Drainage Pipe

Crosspiece

Deadmen

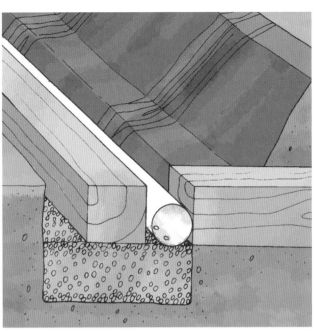

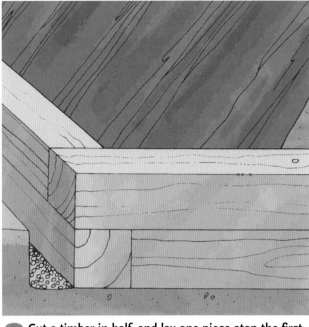

2 Place 4-in. PVC drainage pipe in the trench atop the gravel at the same depth as the first timber course. The holes in the pipe should face downward. Pitch the pipe about ¼ in. per foot to drain, past the end of the wall. Tuck landscape fabric behind the pipe and up the back slope to separate the earth from the gravel backfill.

3 Cut a timber in half, and lay one piece atop the first course, starting at the wall end or corner. This half-timber ensures that the rest of the joints along the length of the wall will be separated by at least a half-timber. Stagger the joints along the entire wall. Spike courses together by driving the galvanized spikes about 2 ft. from each joint.

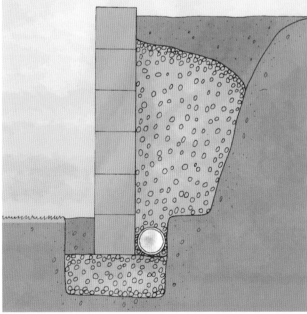

4 Set timbers back ¼ in. from the face of the ones below. This setback, or batter, will help the wall resist the weight of the earth and any groundwater pressure that builds up behind it. To tie the wall into the hillside, install deadmen and crosspieces about 8 ft. apart along the length of the wall. Drill holes, and drive 24-in.-long rebar through the deadmen into the ground.

5 After placing several rows of timbers, repack the earth in front of the wall, and tamp it level with the grade. Also begin backfilling behind the wall with gravel. The fabric filters groundwater behind the wall, preventing silt from blocking up the gravel. Cut rebar 24 in. longer than the wall is high. Drill holes 8 in. on either side of the joints, and drive rebar into the ground.

INTERLOCKING CONCRETE-BLOCK WALLS

project

Interlocking blocks may look like natural stone, and they come in a variety of shapes, colors, and textures. They usually interlock by means of pins, clips, or joints cast into the block. Usually, each course is stepped back slightly from the one beneath to create a batter angle. No mortar or reinforcing bar is required.

TOOLS & MATERIALS

- Work gloves and safety glasses
- Shovel and wheelbarrow
- Soil tamper ▮ Gravel ▮ Retaining wall block
- Spirit level ▮ Perforated drainage pipe
- String and mason's blocks
- Hammer and brick set
- Circular saw with masonry blade (optional)
- Block connectors ▮ Caulking gun
- Adhesive for cap block (if necessary)

1 Because landscape blocks are uniform in size and shape, it is important to place them on a level footing, which can be tamped soil or a compacted sand or gravel base. Begin by laying out and digging the trench to a depth equal to one-half course of blocks plus 3 to 6 in. of depth for the gravel base. Tamp the soil level at the trench bottom.

4 Place 4-in. PVC drainpipe behind the first row of blocks at the same level as the footing material. Drain holes in the pipe face downward. (Indicator stripes on the opposite side of the pipe, if provided, should face up.) The pipe should rest on gravel and slope slightly toward the end of the wall, exiting the trench at its lowest point so that it drains freely.

5 When the base course is complete, begin placing the second row of blocks. Start this course with an end or corner block, or cut a block in half, if necessary, in order to stagger the joints and create a running-bond pattern. Vertical joints that line up will create a weaker bond. Use line blocks, and stretch a level string to be sure the top of this course is even.

2 Place 3 to 6 in. of gravel in the trench. Tamp the gravel well to provide a firm, level base for the wall. If the wall is built on a hillside, a trench stepped to follow the slope of the hill is required. Be sure the entire base row is set below grade, measuring at least one-half the depth of the blocks. This should resist any shifting caused by the pressure of the earth behind them.

3 Lay the first row of blocks in the trench. Try not to disturb the footing material below them. Making the base course straight and level is critical to the entire wall construction. Check frequently at multiple points to see that each block is level, and use a straightedge to be sure that the tops of the blocks are even with one another along the entire row.

6 With the second course in place, backfill with gravel to cover the drainpipe. The pipe may be covered with an optional filter fabric sleeve, or you can use landscape fabric behind the wall. You don't have to worry about weep holes: the blocks are designed to stack closely together with built-in spacing, and the joints between the blocks are open enough to allow water to drain.

7 When necessary, blocks can be cut on site to fit your layout. First, score a cutline on the block with a chisel or brick set or use a circular saw with a masonry blade to cut a shallow groove. Do not attempt to saw completely through the block. Next, use a hammer and mason's chisel, or brick set, to separate the block along the cutline. Continued on next page.

Retaining Walls

Continued from previous page.

8 There are many types of landscape blocks available today, and each may have specific requirements for construction. Always follow the manufacturer's instructions carefully. This product uses sturdy plastic pegs to help align the courses. Simply insert the pegs in the appropriate slots, and line up the blocks when you install the next overlapping course.

9 Pegs also may be installed horizontally to add strength by tying the blocks together along the length of the wall. The pins permanently secure the blocks, but they are loosely fitted, enabling the wall to be easily dismantled or repaired. This method also makes for a strong, resilient wall that allows for some ground movement, unlike rigid mortared walls.

10 As you build the wall, check frequently that the blocks are level and plumb. Most wall systems have a built-in setback, or batter, that helps to reinforce the wall. Some landscape blocks, like these, use pegs to align each course of blocks, while others are shaped with a stepped pattern on top and bottom to automatically provide the right amount of setback.

11 Landscape block systems include cap blocks for a finished appearance. Most cap blocks are cut in a roughly triangular shape that interlock when alternately installed. Cap block faces may be smooth-surfaced or rough to match split-face wall blocks. Exterior-grade adhesive caulk is usually recommended for securing the cap blocks to the wall top.

DRY-LAID STONE WALLS

Dry-laid stones create a natural-looking retaining wall. Construction is similar to building a dry-laid freestanding wall, although the retaining wall usually requires a wider base and a greater batter angle. Generally, the width of the wall at the base should equal at least half the wall height. In most situations, large base stones serve as the wall footing, so no poured-concrete footing is needed.

As with freestanding walls, you must pay careful attention to selecting and fitting the stones for your project.

Depending on the size and shape of your stones, and the wall height, you can build the wall one, two, or even three wythes thick. Lay two stones over one and one stone over two. Use bond stones to tie the wythes together every 4 to 6 feet and at each end of the wall. Ideally, some of these stones should extend behind the wall so that the weight of the earth will hold them in place. The largest, flattest stones are used for the base. It's best to leave the construction of stone retaining walls more than 3 feet tall to experienced stonemasons.

BUILDING A DRY-LAID RETAINING WALL

AFTER EXCAVATING THE SITE, cut and fill to create a space for the wall. Lay out the wall with stakes and strings, and excavate a level trench about twice as wide as the proposed bottom course of stones. Dig the trench deep enough to house the base stones. In wet or unstable soils, dig a deeper trench and add 2 to 3 inches of compacted sand or gravel to promote drainage. Line the cutout area with landscape fabric to keep the gravel you'll put there from clogging.

Select the largest and flattest stones for the base course. Lay them in the trench so that they tilt slightly toward the bank. Use large, flat bond stones at each end of the wall and at 4- to 6-foot intervals along it. Between the bond stones, lay stones one in front of the other to create a double-wythe wall. Long bond stones can extend behind the back of the wall and be cut into the bank to help support the wall. After laying the first course, replace any soil on the front side of the wall, and tamp firmly. Install a perforated drainpipe behind the wall.

Add the Backfill. Place the next course of stones set back slightly from the first course to start the batter angle. Continue to add bond stones, which extend back toward the hillside. To prevent the stones from toppling, begin filling the uphill side of the wall with gravel. Add enough fill to bring the gravel to the same level as the top of the highest stones; then tamp it.

Add Remaining Courses. Build up the remaining courses, stepping the stones slightly back against the slope, staggering joints, and installing bond stones periodically. Fill the gaps with rubble stones. Use a batter gauge to ensure that the wall angles back 1 to 2 inches per 1 foot of height. (See "Make a Batter Gauge," on page 156.) Every one or two courses, add gravel up to the top of the wall, and tamp it. Backfill to within 4 inches of the top of the wall, and cover with topsoil.

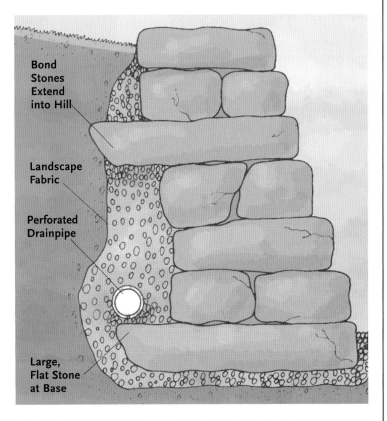

Bond Stones Extend into Hill

Landscape Fabric

Perforated Drainpipe

Large, Flat Stone at Base

Resource Guide

This list of manufacturers and associations is meant to be a general guide to additional industry and product-related sources. It is not intended as a listing of products and manufacturers represented by the photographs in this book.

MANUFACTURERS, DISTRIBUTORS, AND RETAILERS

Acme Brick Co.
P. O. Box 425
Fort Worth, TX 76101
Phone: 800-792-1234 ex. 365
www.brick.com
Manufacturer that designs bricks for architectural and residential projects. Its Web site provides information and masonry designer service to consumers.

Anchor Wall Systems
5959 Baker Rd., Ste. 390
Minnetonka, MN 53345
Phone: 877-295-5415
www.anchorwall.com
Produces a line of interlocking concrete-block wall products. The Web site offers consumer information and project plans.

Artcrete, Inc.
5812 Hwy. 494
Natchitoches, LA 71457
Phone: 318-379-2000
www.artcrete.com
Manufactures faux brick for driveways, paths, and patios.

Bomanite
232 S. Schnoor Ave.
Madera, CA 93637
Phone: 559-673-2411
www.bomanite.com
A manufacturer of stamped and imprinted concrete, as well as accessories, sealers, and concrete curing products.

Boulder Creek Stone Products
8282 Arthur St., NE
Minneapolis, MN 55432
Phone: 800-762-5902
www.bouldercreekstone.com
Manufactures thin brick, floor tile pavers, stone veneer, and accessories.

Endicott Clay Products Co.
P. O. Box 17
Fairbury, NE 68352
Phone: 402-729-3315
www.endicott.com
Designer of commercial, residential, and landscape brick products.

J & N Stone
13729 David Dr.
Grabill, IN 46741
Phone: 260-627-2404
www.jnstone.com
Produces manufactured stone products, including cobblestone, field pavers, and ashlar, among others.

Keystone Retaining Walls
4444 W. 78th St.
Minneapolis, MN 55435
Phone: 800-747-8971
www.keystonewalls.com
Offers a broad line of retaining wall products, from residential to commercial units.

Stone Info.com
8711 E. Pinnacle Peak Rd.
Scottsdale, AZ 85255
Phone: 480-502-5354
www.stoneinfo.com
A division of KD Resources, the Web site offers valuable information to construction professionals.

Taylor Clay Products
P. O. Box 2128
Salisbury, NC 28145
Phone: 704-636-2411
www.taylorclay.com
Manufactures a wide variety of face bricks in many different colors and shapes in both standard and custom sizes.

Unilock
Unilock-New York
51 International Blvd.
Brewster, NY 10509
Phone: 800-864-5625
www.unilock.com
Manufactures products such as standard pavers, textured pavers, and retaining and garden wall blocks.

Versa-lok Retaining Wall Systems
6348 Hwy. 36
Oakdale, MN 55128
Phone: 651-770-3166
www.versa-lok.com
Produces interlocking-block wall systems for residential and commercial uses. The company provides installation tips and landscape ideas.

ASSOCIATIONS

American Institute of Architects (AIA)

1735 New York Ave., NW
Washington, DC 20006-5292
Phone: 800-242-3837
www.aia.org
Offers a Web site with up-to-date news, an event calendar, and other information. The main purpose of the AIA's Web site is to help professionals, but the site also helps consumers locate architects.

The Brick Industry Association

11490 Commerce Park Dr.
Reston, VA 20191-1525
Phone: 703-620-0010
www.bia.org
Promotes manufacturers' and distributors' interests. Its Web site provides free information to homeowners.

Cast Stone Institute

10 W. Kimball St.
Winder, GA 30680-2535
Phone: 770-868-5909
www.caststone.org
Nonprofit trade organization that aims to improve the quality of cast stone.

Ceramic Tile Institute of America, Inc. (CTIOA)

12061 W. Jefferson Blvd.
Culver City, CA 90230-6219
Phone: 310-574-7800
www.ctioa.org
Supports the expanded use of ceramic tile. Its Web site provides tile information for consumers.

Concrete Foundations Association of North America

107 First St. W.
P. O. Box 204
Mount Vernon, IA 52314
Phone: 319-895-6940
www.cfawalls.org
Provides educational resources to engineers, contractors, producers, concrete suppliers, and consumers in both the U.S. and Canada.

The Hearth, Patio, and Barbecue Association (HPBA)

1601 N. Kent St., Ste. 1001
Arlington, VA 22209
Phone: 703-522-0086
www.hpba.org
Promotes the hearth-products industry through information to consumers. Its members include manufacturers, retailers, installation firms, and distributors.

Interlocking Concrete Pavement Institute (ICPI)

1444 I St. NW, Ste. 700
Washington, DC 20005-2210
Phone: 202-712-9036
www.icpi.org
A membership organization that educates homeowners, designers, and contractors about concrete paving products.

The International Masonry Institute

42 East St.
Annapolis, MD 21401
Phone: 800-464-0988
www.imiweb.org
Offers design assistance and information to the public. It also helps consumers find professional craftworkers.

National Association of Home Builders Research Center

400 Prince George's Blvd.
Upper Marlboro, MD 20774
Phone: 800-638-8556
www.nahbrc.org
Provides information on housing technology.

Portland Cement Association

5420 Old Orchard Rd.
Skokie, IL 60077
Phone: 847-966-6200
www.portcement.org
Provides handbooks, resources, and research reports to improve the quality of concrete construction.

Glossary

Actual dimensions The measured dimensions of a masonry unit.

Aggregate Crushed stone, gravel, or other material added to cement to make concrete or mortar. Gravel and crushed stone are considered course aggregate; sand is considered fine aggregate.

Air-entrained concrete Mixture that contains tiny air pockets that allow moisture to freeze and thaw without damaging the structure. Common in cold climates.

Backfill Sand, gravel, pea stone, crushed stone, slag, or cinders used for filling around foundations or piping. In general, to backfill is to replace earth in a trench or around a foundation.

Bat A brick that is cut in half lengthwise.

Bed joint Horizontal masonry joint, opposed to a vertical masonry joint (head joint). Also called beds.

Brick Clay that is molded to shape and fired at high temperatures in a large kiln or oven. The color of the natural clay determines the color of the brick.

Broom finish The texture created when a concrete surface is stroked with a stiff broom while the concrete is still curing.

Buttering Placing mortar on a masonry unit using a trowel.

Collar joint The vertical joint between wythes.

Concave joint A masonry joint that is recessed and formed in mortar. A curved steel jointing tool is used to make a concave joint.

Concrete Fresh concrete is a semifluid mixture of portland cement, sand (fine aggregate), gravel, or crushed stone.

Concrete block A masonry unit that consists of an outside shell with a hollow center that is divided by two or three vertical webs. The ends of the unit may have flanges that accept mortar and join with adjacent blocks, or they may have smooth ends for corners and the ends of walls.

Concrete pavers Commonly used for patios and walks, concrete pavers come in a number of shapes and colors and are designed to be laid in a sand base without mortar; some interlock to form repeating patterns.

Control joints Special joints, also called "contraction joints," that are tooled into the surface to allow concrete to crack in straight lines at planned locations.

Curing The process by which concrete becomes solid and develops strength. Proper moisture reduces cracking and shrinkage.

Darby A long tool used for smoothing the surface of a concrete slab.

Edging joints The rounded edges of a pour that are resistant to cracking.

Excavation To dig out earth or soil so that a slab will be supported by a subgrade that is hard, uniformly graded, and well drained.

Expansion joint A planned break in the continuous surface of a structure into which a compressible material has been placed. The material absorbs pressure when the surface expands when heated. This joint prevents buckling or crumbling of the surface. Expansion joints are required wherever dissimilar materials adjoin because they will expand and contract at different rates.

Face brick A type of brick used when consistency in appearance is required. A batch of face brick will be quite uniform in color, size, texture, and face structure.

Flagstone pattern A simulated pattern that has been "carved" into concrete.

Floating The process of smoothing the surface of a pour with a float made of steel, aluminum, magnesium, or wood. This action drives large aggregate below the surface.

Footing Support for garden walls of brick, block, or stone. Generally made of concrete, footings are also used for stairs and are usually located below the local frost line to avoid problems from frost heave.

Formwork The forms or molds that contain and shape wet concrete. Forms are usually built from lumber; plywood is used for curved sections.

Frost heave Shifting or upheaval of the ground resulting from alternate freezing and thawing of water in the soil.

Frost line The maximum depth to which soil freezes in the winter. The local building department can provide information of the frost-line depth in your area.

Head joints Vertical mortar joints between bricks.

Header The position in a wall in which the brick is rotated 90 degrees from the stretcher position so that the end is facing out.

Hydration The process of cement particles chemically reacting with water. When this happens, the concrete hardens into a durable material.

Mason's line A length of twine that is held at each end by an L-shaped block. The line can be stretched tight and is used as a straightedge guide, permitting the mason to check the evenness of the course being laid.

Mortar A mixture of cementitious materials, fine aggregate, and water. Mortar is used to bond bricks or blocks.

Nominal dimensions The dimensions of a masonry unit plus one mortar joint.

Portland cement A mixture of burned lime, iron, silica, and alumina. This mixture is put through a kiln and then is ground into a fine powder and packaged for sale. The cement is the same color as the gray limestone quarried near Portland, England.

Prepackaged concrete mix A mix that combines cement, sand, and gravel in the correct proportions and requires only the addition of water to create fresh concrete.

Ready-mix concrete Wet concrete that is transported from a concrete supplier. The concrete is ready to pour.

Rebar Reinforcing bar (called "rebar" for short), is used for concrete that will carry a heavy load, such as footings, foundation walls, columns, and pilasters.

Reinforcing mesh Steel wires woven or welded into a grid of 6 or 10 inch squares. The mesh is primarily used in flatwork, such as walks and patios.

Retaining walls A wall built to hold back a slope. Retaining walls are used to create terraces in sloping ground.

Rowlock A brick laid on its face edge horizontally so that the face is visible in the wall.

Sailor A brick laid on its end vertically so that the end is visible in the wall.

Screeding Using a straight 2x4 moved from one end of a concrete pour to the other to strike off excess concrete and level the surface.

Segregation A condition that results when the concrete is overworked—such as when trying to remove air bubbles—and the water separates and rises to the top.

Soap A brick that is halved in width.

Soldier A brick standing upright with the edge facing out.

Split A brick that is halved in height.

Steel reinforcement Reinforcing mesh or rebar that is used to strengthen concrete.

Stretcher A brick that is laid lengthwise in the course.

Stucco A cementitious material made of sand, portland cement, lime, and water. Stucco is applied in thin layers to provide a durable finish for walls.

Troweling Finishing the concrete after it has been screeded. This finishing step is for interior concrete applications and concrete without air-entrainment.

Weep hole A hole in a retaining wall that allows water to seep through.

Wythe The vertical section of a wall that is equal to the width of the masonry unit.

Index

Index

Index

Photo Credits

Illustrations by Ron Carboni, Craig Franklin, Paul M. Schumm.

Roger Wade, builder: Roth Construction Mark Lohman Jessie Walker Mark Lohman Mark Lohman, design: Key Vision Interiors; John Casey/Dreamstime.com; Olson Photographic, LLC, builder: Olson Development LLC, New Canaan, CT Olson Photographic, LLC; & Mark Lohman; Tony Giammarino/Giammarino & Dworkin Mark Lohman Olson Photographic, LLC, builder: Pembrook/Caledon, Wilton, CT Mark Lohman, design: Kathryne Designs Tony Giammarino/Giammarino & Dworkin; Mark Lohman Olson Photographic, LLC, design/builder: Timberdale Homes, Bethel, CT & Mark Lohman, design: G. Grisamore Design Inc.; Tony Giammarino/Giam-marino & Dworkin Mark Lohman Olson Photographic, LLC, builder: Avonridge, Avon, CT Mark Lohman Olson Photographic, LLC, design: Innerspace Electronics, Portchester, NY Olson Photographic, LLC, builder: Coastal Point Development, Greenwich, CT, design: TPA Design Group, New Haven, CT Mark Lohman, design: Harte Brownlee & Assoc. Mark Lohman; Tria Giovan & Roger Wade, architect: Ellis Nunn & Associates, builder: Teton Heritage Builders; Olson Photographic, LLC; Mark Lohman Olson Photographic, LLC Olson Photographic, LLC, builder: LS Construction, New Fairfield, CT, design/builder: Timberdale Homes, Bethel, CT Mark Lohman, design: Pamela Volante Design Mark Lohman Olson Photographic, LLC, architect: Nautilus Architecture, Deep River, CT Olson Photographic, LLC; Olson Photographic, LLC, builder: LS Construction, New Fairfield, CT Roger Wade, builder: Kenneth Bealer Homes, Inc. Brian Grant/Dreamstime.com Roger Wade, architect: McLaughlin & Associates; Roger Wade, design: Moss Creek Design, builder: Barber Custom Homes; Kathy Wismer, stylist: Susan Andrews; Tony Giammarino/Giammarino& Dworkin Kathy Wismer, stylist: Susan Andrews Roger Wade Jessie Walker Mark Lohman Kathy Wismer, stylist: Susan Andrews; Olson Photographic, LLC, design/architect: William Earls Architect, Wilton, CT Tony Giammarino/Giammarino& Dworkin Olson Photographic, LLC, Mark Lohman; John Parsekian/CH Mark Lohman Mark Lohman Jerry Pavia John Parsekian/CH Mark Lohman; & Brian C. Nieves/CH; John Parsekian/CH Mark Lohman Olson Photographic, LLC, design/architect: Paul Shainberg Architects, Rye, NY John Parsekian/CH Jessie Walker; Jerry Pavia Jerry Pavia Jessie Walker; Alan & Linda Detrick, design: The New York Botanical Gardens John Parsekian/ CH Mark Lohman Olson Photographic, LLC, builder: Olson Development LLC, New Canaan, CT Jerry Pavia Mark Lohman; Jerry Pavia Mark Lohman Brian C. Nieves/CH John Parsekian/CH Charles Mann; John Parsekian/CH Olson Photographic, LLC, builder: Coastal Construction Management, Mystic, CT, builder: Olson Development LLC, New Canaan, CT Olson Photographic, LLC John Parsekian/CH Olson Photographic, LLC, builder: Country Club Homes, Wilton, CT Mark Lohman; Merle Henkenius Brian C. Nieves/CH John Parsekian/CH & John Parsekian/CH; Patricia Marroquin/Dreamstime.com Roger Wade, builder: Roth Construction Bruce Shippee/Dreamstime.com Tony Giammarino/ Giammarino & Dworkin, design: Gracestreet.com; Olson Photographic, LLC; & Mark Lohman Olson Photographic, LLC, builder: Country Club Homes courtesy of Bomanite; Mark Lohman Kathy Wismer, stylist: Susan Andrews Mark Lohman Mark Lohman, design: Barclay Butera Inc.; & Brian C. Nieves/CH; John Parsekian/CH Mark Lohman, design: Key Vision Interiors Alan & Linda Detrick; Olson Photographic, LLC, builder: VAS Construction, Wilton, CT Mark Samu John Casey/ Dreamstime.com Brian C. Nieves/CH , & Brian C. Nieves/ CH; John Parsekian/CH Olson Photographic, LLC; John Parsekian/CH Peter Tata Robert Greenspan, stylist: Susan Andrews Mark Lohman, design: Janet Louise Lohman Garden Design John Parsekian/CH courtesy of Bomanite; & courtesy of Artcrete Inc. John Parsekian/CH Jerry Pavia; John Parsekian/CH Jerry Pavia; John Parsekian/CH Tony Giammarino/Giammarino & Dworkin, builder: Chip Spitzer Construction Jerry Pavia John Parsekian/CH Mark Samu; John Parsekian/CH John Parsekian/CH Jerry Pavia Olson Photographic, LLC, design/architect: Paul Shainberg Architects, Rye, NY; Brian C. Nieves/ CH; John Parsekian/CH John Parsekian/CH Mark Lohman; John Parsekian/CH Mark Lohman Olson Photographic, LLC, design/architect: Terry Architecture, North Branford, CT John Parsekian/ CH Lynne Furrer/Dreamstime.com; John Parsekian/CH John Parsekian/CH Tria Giovan, design: Carl Pasota John Parsekian/CH Tria Giovan, design: Carl Pasota Mark Lohman Tony Giamma-rino/Giammarino & Dworkin Shannon Workman/Dreamstime.com Jessie Walker Elena Elisseeva/ Dreamstime.com Tony Giammarino/Giammarino & Dworkin, design: design: Janice Hall Nuckolls Jessie Walker Olson Photographic, LLC, design/builder: Timberdale Homes, Bethel, CT; John Parsekian/CH Alan & Linda Detrick; Tony Giammarino/Giam-marino & Dworkin, design: Keystone Retaining Wall Systems Olson Photographic, LLC, builder: Hemingway Construction, Greenwich, CT John Parsekian/CH Mark Lohman, design: G. Grisamore Design Inc. Mark Lohman Peter Tata Olson Photographic, LLC.

Metric Equivalents

Length

1 inch	25.4mm
1 foot	0.3048m
1 yard	0.9144m
1 mile	1.61km

Area

1 square inch	645mm²
1 square foot	0.0929m²
1 square yard	0.8361m²
1 acre	4046.86m²
1 square mile	2.59km²

Volume

1 cubic inch	16.3870cm³
1 cubic foot	0.03m³
1 cubic yard	0.77m³

Common Lumber Equivalents

Sizes: Metric cross sections are so close to their U.S. sizes, as noted below, that for most purposes they may be considered equivalents.

Dimensional lumber	1 x 2	19 x 38mm
	1 x 4	19 x 89mm
	2 x 2	38 x 38mm
	2 x 4	38 x 89mm
	2 x 6	38 x 140mm
	2 x 8	38 x 184mm
	2 x 10	38 x 235mm
	2 x 12	38 x 286mm
Sheet sizes	4 x 8 ft.	1200 x 2400mm
	4 x 10 ft.	1200 x 3000mm
Sheet thicknesses	¼ in.	6mm
	⅜ in.	9mm
	½ in.	12mm
	¾ in.	19mm
Stud/joist spacing	16 in. o.c.	400mm o.c.
	24 in. o.c.	600mm o.c.

Capacity

1 fluid ounce	29.57mL
1 pint	473.18mL
1 quart	0.95L
1 gallon	3.79L

Weight

1 ounce	28.35g
1 pound	0.45kg

Temperature

Fahrenheit = Celsius x 1.8 + 32

Celsius = Fahrenheit - 32 x ⁵⁄₉

Nail Size and Length

Penny Size	Nail Length
2d	1"
3d	1¼"
4d	1½ "
5d	1¾"
6d	2"
7d	2¼"
8d	2½"
9d	2¾"
10d	3"
12d	3¼"
16d	3½"

Have a home improvement, decorating, or gardening project? Look for these and other fine Creative Homeowner books wherever books are sold.

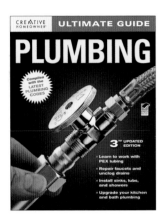

The complete manual for plumbing projects. Over 775 color photos and illustrations. 304 pp.; 8^1/$_2$" × 10^7/$_8$"

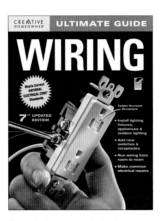

Electrical systems in basic terms. Over 950 color photos, illustrations. 304 pp.; 8^1/$_2$" × 10^7/$_8$"

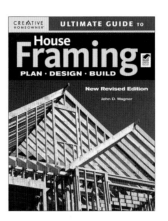

Walks you through the framing basics. Over 650 photos and illustrations. 240 pp.; 8^1/$_2$" × 10^7/$_8$"

The ultimate home-improvement reference manual. Over 300 step-by-step projects. 608 pp.; 9" × 10^7/$_8$"

Complete source book for molding trim. 1,000+ color photos and illos. 256 pp.; 8^1/$_2$" × 10^7/$_8$"

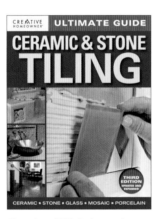

Complete DIY tile instruction. Over 550 color photos and illustrations. 240 pp.; 8^1/$_2$" × 10^7/$_8$"

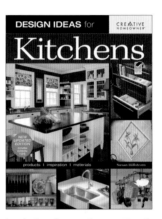

Inspiration for creating an attractive, up-to-date kitchen. Over 500 color photos. 224 pp.; 8^1/$_2$" × 10^7/$_8$"

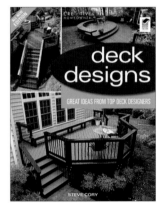

Great deck ideas from top designers. Over 450 color photos. 240 pp.; 8^1/$_2$" x 10^7/$_8$"

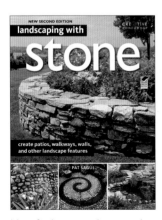

Ideas for incorporating stone into the landscape. Over 335 color photos. 224 pp.; 8^1/$_2$" × 10^7/$_8$"

Tips on gardening methods and selecting plants. Over 450 photos and illos. 256 pp.; 8^1/$_2$" × 10^7/$_8$"

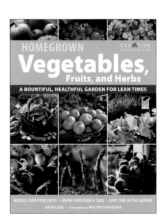

Grow your own vegetables, fruits, and herbs. Over 275 photos and illustrations. 192 pp. 8^1/$_2$" × 10^7/$_8$"

The quick and easy way to grow fruit and vegetables. Over 300 color photos and illos. 384 pp.; 8^1/$_2$" × 10^7/$_8$"

For more information and to order direct, visit our Web site at **www.creativehomeowner.com**